Nawab of Bhopal Muhammad Siddiq Hasan

An Interpreter of Wahabiism

Nawab of Bhopal Muhammad Siddiq Hasan
An Interpreter of Wahabism
ISBN/EAN: 9783337350956

Printed in Europe, USA, Canada, Australia, Japan

Cover: Foto ©Thomas Meinert / pixelio.de

More available books at **www.hansebooks.com**

AN

INTERPRETER OF WAHABIISM,

BY THE

NAWÁB WÁLÁJÁH AMÍR-UL-MULK,

SAYYAD MUHAMMAD SIDDIḲ HASAN
KHÁN BAHADÚR,

TRANSLATED FROM THE ORIGINAL URDU,

AND EDITED BY

SAYYAD AKBAR 'ALAM,

THIRD ASSISTANT TO THE SECOND MINISTER OF

BHOPÁL.

CALCUTTA:
PUBLISHED BY THE AUTHOR AT BHOPÁL.
1884.

TRANSLATOR'S PREFACE.

ERRATA.

Page	line		for		read
1,	10	,,	pour in	read	pour
8,	18	,,	fourth	,,	forth
14,	2	,,	Adala-tul-Masail	read	Adilla-tul-Masnil.
15,	7	,,	htose	read	those
17,	12	,,	the	,,	a
37,	19	,,	Aba Daúd	,,	Abú Daúd
37,	28	,,	the	,,	a
41,	31	,,	from the	,,	from
51,	6	,,	Almgiri	,,	Alamgiri
51,	29	,,	both the	,,	both
77,	7	,,	or	,,	nor have I
86,	14	,,	leadars	,,	leaders
91,	32	,,	do not exist	,,	exist
92,	24	,,	Pikah	,,	Fikah
94,	1	,,	bave	,,	have
101,	3	,,	and bribery	,,	bribery
102,	26	,,	perpetuating	,,	perpetrating

can even approach the author in the profundity and depth of his knowledge of Arabic literature. He is also a great Arabic, Persian and Urdu poet. He has composed sixty-three works, in prose and verse, of various sizes, on different subjects, within a remarkably short time; and I can hardly recollect any *alim* who has done the same.

TRANSLATOR'S PREFACE.

I received the commands of Her Highness the Nawab Shahjahan Begam, G. C. S. I., C. I. E., Ruler of Bhopál, to translate this work. Accordingly, I undertook the translation and devoted only such portions of my time to it as could be spared from my official duties. It was commenced in April and finished about the 25th August 1883. I have tried to make the translation literal.

Munshi Muhammad Abdul Aziz, formerly First Assistant to the Second Minister of Bhopál, rendered me material assistance in the translation of this work. He translated the fifth chapter entirely himself, and revised the whole manuscript along with me, suggesting many improved alterations.

The author of this work, Nawab Sayyad Muhammad Siddik Hasan Khán Bahadur, Consort of Her Highness the Begam of Bhopál, is a man of vast literary acquirements. I doubt if there is any *alim* in India at the present day who can even approach the author in the profundity and depth of his knowledge of Arabic literature. He is also a great Arabic, Persian and Urdu poet. He has composed sixty-three works, in prose and verse, of various sizes, on different subjects, within a remarkably short time; and I can hardly recollect any *alim* who has done the same.

In recognition of his princely position, acquired mostly by personal qualifications and partly by good fortune, Government has conferred upon him the title of Nawab Wálájáh Amir-ul-Mulk and fixed for him a personal salute of seventeen guns in British territories. Nevertheless, he is courteous and unceremonious in his intercourse with men of all classes. He is accessible to all men, high and low, and has a kind word to say to every one. These are things which are not commonly met with in men of similar rank.

He possesses a handsome body and a handsome countenance. During this year's *Id* festival, I observed with a scrutinizing eye, the features of the thousands of men that had assembled in the *Idgah* at Shahjahanábád, Bhopál, but none did I find so regularly and handsomely built, and yet so simply and unostentatiously clad as the Nawab Wálájáh Amir-ul-Mulk.

The Nawab is unpretending and averse to all sorts of pomp and ceremonies, the usual concomitants of wealth and power and characteristics of the magnates of India. He is simple in his dress, manners and all his surroundings. The way in which he receives his visitors whoever they be and the bewitchingly unceremonious mode of his talking to them, are sure to impress them with the ideas of his good nature and the sincerity of his heart.

I have seen the Nawab Wálájáh perform his prayers, have prayed with him, have gone through some of his theological compilations and have heard him talk on different occasions; but never have I observed anything tending to Wahabiism in his speech, his writings or his modes of prayer. Persons holding Wahabi inclinations have a certain way of prayer that cannot long conceal them. The Nawab Wálájáh says his prayers just like the generality of the Mahomedans. Besides this, he is perfectly liberal in his views of religion, and a toleration of it is an abiding principle in the reign of Her Highness the Begam of Bhopál. However, malicious and interested persons grudging his good luck and the dignity to which he has attained, have not left the Nawab Wálájáh undisturbed in the enjoyment of home and social comforts. They caused to be published, some time ago, in one of the Indian Newspapers, the report that the Nawab held Wahabi doctrines—a charge not only ridiculous but altogether groundless. They did not stop even here. They sent anonymous letters to the British Authorities with a view to prejudice their minds against the Nawab and cast a slur upon his well-earned reputation. But their machinations proved of no avail. Government did not pay any heed to their reports, and they were consequently obliged to keep their silence.

The Nawab Wálájáh is in possession of letters from such personages as Lord Northbrook, Lord Lytton, Lord Ripon, General Sir Henry Daly, Sir Donald Stewart, the late Mr. Blochmann, &c., &c., and the British officers that have happened to be connected with the State of Bhopál as Political Agents during the time of the Nawab, and also such as have chanced to make his acquaintance. Some of these letters are complimentary, some on the enquiries of health and return of good wishes, some in acknowledgment of hospitality received at Bhopál, some in reference to the

Nawab's literary productions and some testifying to his good sense and sound judgment,—in fact, all indicating friendly relations of the Nawab with their several writers. I intend to quote here only a few letters from those British officers that have served here as Political Agents and who, by their position and official connection with the affairs of this State, and frequent interviews with the Nawab himself, have had better opportunities than any other of the corresponding gentlemen, of forming an estimate of his administrative abilities.

Colonel Kincaid, the present Political Agent of Bhopál thus writes to Her Highness the Nawab Shahjahan Begam:—

"MY DEAR FRIEND,—I have great pleasure to forward to Your Highness the accompanying letter, the Agent, Governor-General, Colonel Bannerman, has given to me for that purpose. Mrs. Kincaid and myself join in wishing you a happy new year as is our custom, and trust the Nawab Wálájáh may have quite recovered his health.

"Your Highness's officials have most assuredly done their best under Your Highness's orders to make the Agent Governor-General's path smooth, whilst he and his family have been travelling through the Bhopál Districts. And everything has shewn Your Highness's anxiety to assist towards the comfort of his Camp, and he is very much pleased. And not only did he express this to me, but also remarked that it appeared to him that Your Highness's Consort the Nawab Sahib most ably seconded your efforts."

"*Bhopál, 11th May,* 1879.

"*To the Nawab Wálájáh Sayyad Muhammad Siddík Hasan Khan Bahadur, Amir-ul-Mulk.*

"MY FRIEND,

"I have received the two Arabic works, which you have composed, and which you have been good enough to present to me. I beg to offer my best thanks for this token of your friendship. It is fitting that persons of exalted rank should provide those who are not so favoured by Providence with the means of acquiring knowledge, and I trust that you will at times find leisure from the duties which your high position entails upon you, to compose other works which will afford information to those who are desirous of knowledge.

"I remain,
"Your friend and well-wisher,
"W. F. PRIDEAUX,
"*Political Agent.*"

"*Sehore, 31st September,* 1878.

"MY DEAR FRIEND,
"I write to wish you may acquire happiness and prosperity during the coming year. May you see many more new years, and may each bring the fulfilment of all your wishes. With every good wish,
"Believe me
"Your most sincere friend,
"W. OSBORNE,
"*Political Agent.*"

"*Sehore, 2nd April,* 1879.

"MY DEAR FRIEND,
"I could not say all I wished this morning so must write it. I am leaving Bhopál, and I must, before I go, thank you and all the members of your family. May God bless and keep you and all those near and dear to you, and may we both be spared to meet again. I hope some day to return to Bhopál again in a higher position, when I shall hope to find that the good reputation of the Bhopál Rulers and State have continued to increase. Bhopál has been our home for many years; our children have been born here, and I cannot leave it without very many regrets. The friendship between us has grown and increased steadily since we first visited it, and will, therefore, I hope, last for ever. With earnest and best wishes.
"Believe me,
"Ever your most sincere friend,
"W. OSBORNE,
"*Political Agent.*"

"*Sehore, 26th March* 1883.

"*To the Nawab Wálájáh of Bhopál.*

"MY DEAR SIR,

"I write a few lines to thank you for the good advice you gave Her Highness the Begam concerning the proposed construction of the road from the Parbati river to Sehore. I have forwarded a translation of Her Highness's communication to Indore, and stated that I have every reason to believe, that after the State be released from its heavy Railway payments, the funds necessary would be ordinarily supplied; because Her Highness understands better than most princes, that the real interests of herself and ryots would be benefitted by extended communication, the construction of Railway feeders. I am aware also, that on these matters your opinion and advice is sound, so much so, that I also mentioned, that I felt confident, that after the Railway is finished, Her Highness would take into favourable consideration the proposal to construct a Railway feeder road from the pargana of Bairasya to Bhopál. Her Highness and yourself have now ascertained that nothing will more derive steady payments of revenue in this large wheat tract than opening up facilities of carriage to the Port of embarkation for export of this commodity; thus keeping high prices and enabling the ryot to pay his rent even though other crops may suffice. With our regards to Her Highness and yourself,

"Believe me,
"Your sincere friend,
"W. KINCAID,
"*Political Agent.*"

"*Sehore, 23rd October,* 1882.

"MY DEAR NAWAB SAHIB,

"Pray permit me to offer my congratulations to you on the occasion of 'Eed' and wish you many happy years to enjoy its festivities. I know the day to be a very important day in Islám, and therefore pray accept my acknowledgments with good wishes also to the members of your family,

"I remain,
"Dear Nawab Sahib,
"W. KINCAID,
"*Political Agent.*"

Colonel H. Moore who, some time ago, came here in the suite of His Excellency the Commander-in-Chief, and who, during his stay here seems to have formed a warm acquaintance with the Nawab Consort, writes to him from Simla under date the 12th June 1883, in the following words:—

"MY DEAR NAWAB,

"I have been away from Simla for the last six months, else would ere this have acknowledged receipt of your very kind letter of the 14th May which I found waiting here for me on my return. It is very pleasant to think that you have not forgotten one who now considers himself an old friend; and believe me, I often think of the very pleasant days I spent at Bhopál and the great kindness we all received from Her Highness, yourself and all connected with the Bhopál State. His Excellency the Commander-in-Chief has desired me to thank you very much for enquiring after his health and Sir Donald Stewart is glad to think that you are quite well. All those who had the good fortune to accompany the Commander-in-Chief on his visit to Bhopál, have most pleasant recollections of their stay at Bhopál, and if they knew I was writing to you, would most certainly desire to be remembered to you. Pray remember me very kindly to Her Highness the Begam and all friends in your city, and with every good wish for your long life and happiness,

"Believe me always,
"Your sincere friend,
"H. MOORE, COL.

"P. S. I have read the books you were good enough to give me with great interest, and think your Highness deserves high praise for your valuable contributions to the literature of this country.

"H. MOORE, COL."

It would not be out of place to extract here a portion from the history of Bhopál that deals with the circumstances attending the author's marriage with Her Highness the Nawab Shahjahan Begam, G. C. S. I., C. I. E., and his subsequent investiture with the *khilat* and title of Nawab Wálájáh Amir-ul-Mulk. Her Highness the Begam, the author of the history writes:—

"On the occasion of my visit to Calcutta, to pay my homage to the Duke of Edinburgh, second son of Her Majesty the Queen, (may her reign be enduring,) Colonel Thompson, the Political Agent of Bhopál, who accompanied me, spoke to me, advising me to marry again to get a helpmate to share the burden of Government; and this advice was repeated to me by Colonel Richard John Meade, Agent to the Governor-General for Central India, on the occasion of our meeting. To this I replied that second marriages were not forbidden by my religion, but that I had not up to that time met with a fitting partner. On my return to Bhopál from Calcutta, I pondered over the advice of these gentlemen, and that advice was in accordance with the mandates of Almighty God, who very strongly in His holy Scriptures enjoins the marriage of widows, and the practice of the marriage of widows also prevails throughout the Musalmán population of Arabia, Turkey, Persia, Turania and Central Asia. Therefore, considering that the advice and admonition of both God and man pointed the same way, I determined to marry some suitable person, agreeable and popular with high and low; and when Colonel Thompson came to Bhopál, to take part in the rejoicings at the Nashra of my beloved daughter (the light of my eyes, may she long be spared!), I thought it proper to openly ask for the sanction of the Governor-General to this fitting act. On the 8th of May, 1871 A. D., or 7th Safar, 1288 A. H., I received an English letter from Colonel John William Willoughby Osborne, C. B., Political Agent, in which he said that he had great pleasure in sending to me a letter from the Foreign Secretary, regarding my proposed marriage, and that he should be much pleased to see me married again. The purport of the enclosed letter was, that His Excellency the Governor-General saw no objection to the Begam's marrying a suitable person, if she wished to do so, but that it would be as well if she consulted the chief persons of her State. Accordingly, with the concurrence of the members of my family and the officers of this State, I made choice of Sayyad Siddík Hasan Khan. This gentleman had been for seventeen years in the service of this State, and was for a long time Munshi to my sainted mother, the Nawab Sikandar Begam, who, appreciating his learning and good qualities, which were second to no other Munshi in Bhopál, appointed him superintendent of the Annals of Bhopál. Next he was placed at the head of the Educational Department, with authority over the Masters of the Sulemani and other Schools, after which the titles of Mir Dabír and Khan were conferred on him, and he was appointed my Secretary. He evinced great ability, honesty, and rapidity in the performance of the duties entrusted to him; one day's work was never put off to the next, and all the officers of the State and my relations approved of his character. This gentleman showed both originality and application, and was complete master of Arabic, Persian, and good-breeding, composition and other sciences. In point of family he was a Sayyad of descent from Fatima, reckoned the best blood among all Muhammadans, and many works on religious subjects, of which he is the author or compiler, have attained a wide reputation. Since he has lived in this State, he has never been fined, nor has fault been found with him for any irregularity, as has been the case with other servants of the State, but he received praise from my sainted mother, and was always given up to study. His father's name was Sayyad Aulád Hasan, of Bokhara and Kanouj, and his grandfather's name Nawáb Sayyad Aulád Alí Khán Bahádur "Anwar Jang," who was one of the principal nobles and renowned jaghirdars of the Government of Nizam-ul-Mulk Asaf Jáh, Ruler of Haidarabad in the Deccan, and nearly related to Amir Shams-ul-Umra, from whom he held a fief worth five lakhs of rupees per annum, and had command of 1,000 cavalry and infantry, and the villages of Manbhali, Mislkhera, and Bimalkhera,

&c., were assigned to him for an estate. His great-grandfather, Sayyad Azízullah, was first cousin to Nawáb Abul Fateh Khan Shams-ul-umra, and his pedigree leads up to Sayyad Jalál of Bokhara " Makhdúm Jahániyán Jahán Gasht." Sayyad Azízullah was one of the great nobles and relatives of the Nizam-ul-Mulk, a lord of territory and of an army. He died in the 90th year of his age, on the 20th Shawal 1279 A. H., and his son has succeeded to his title.

"Suffice it to say that I followed the mandates of the holy Korán and the counsels of English officers, and put an end to evil report, because it was considered improper in the eyes of the world for me to be alone with a stranger and he not my husband, and it often happened that, in the conduct of State affairs, it was absolutely necessary for my Secretary and myself to be alone together. According to the above advice and the dictates of true religion, in the presence of the Madár-ul-Mahám Muhammad Jamáluddin Khán, First Minister of the State of Bhopál, and Shaikh Zain-ul-Abidín Kázi of the State of Bhopál, and other learned doctors and State officers, in a public Darbár held for the purpose, I plighted my troth to the Sayyad Sáhib, and we were married. The news was, according to the established practice of the State, communicated to Colonel Osborne, C. B., Political Agent in Bhopál. On the 30th June, 1871 the following reply was received from that gentleman: 'Your Highness was formerly apprised of the permission accorded to you to marry again by His Excellency the Governor-General, and a letter from the Foreign Secretary to that effect was communicated to you. It is gratifying to the Government to hear that you have satisfactorily carried out your intention.'

"My present husband has been raised to an equality in rank and dignity with the late Nawab Baki Muhammad Khan. The pay attaching to the office of Mír Dabír had been hitherto fixed at Rs 4,931-11. The office of Mótimid-ul-Mahám or Second Minister of State, had been vacant since Saturday the 1st Shaban 1286 A. H., or the 6th of October, 1869 A. D., the date of the death of Raja Krishen Rám; the emoluments of this office consist of an estate worth Rs. 24,000 a year, of which Rs. 6,000 had been continued to the heirs of the deceased Raja, and the rest had lapsed to the State. The office of Mír Dabír was abolished, and the pay transferred to the office of the Second Minister, to which an addition of Rs. 1,068-5-0 was made from the State revenue. The total amounting to Rs. 24,000 per annum, together with the title of Mótimid-ul-Mahám and the office of Second Minister, were conferred upon Sayyad Muhammad Siddik Hasan Khan on Monday the 21st Rabiulákhír, 1288 A. H., or the 2nd July, 1871, with a *khilat*, comprising nine suits of new clothes and five sets of jewels, an umbrella, a banner, a chowri, a horse, an elephant, and a palanquin; in all twenty-four articles, valued at Rs. 21,053-2-6, were conferred upon him in a public Darbar in the presence of the chief officers of the State and my relatives. With the view of showing high and low the honour he had received, I directed him to go forth from my Hall of Audience, mounted on his elephant, surrounded with the pomp and circumstance of his rank, to his own house. He was entrusted with all the duties which the former Second Minister used to carry on in my late mother's time, and was caused by me to administer the office before me in the same manner. Intimation of this matter was sent to the Political Agent in Bhopál in due course, and on the 31st of July 1871 he signified his approval of my excellent arrangements.

" The speech which the Sayyad Sáhib delivered in Darbár on this occasion, is as follows:—" My thanks are due to the All Merciful Providence, by whom the loyalty, truth, industry, and zeal of the servant in the interests of an appreciative, enlightened, liberal and benevolent master, are universally held to be reasons for the elevation of the faithful; and more particularly my thanks are due to Him for making me a partaker in the gracious and generous bounty of the noble and illustrious Chief, in whose boundless benevolence and infinite consideration, not only all present at this Darbár participate, but also many residents of distant cities, and all the inhabitants of the territories of Bhopál are grateful for her kindness. Benedictions and blessings on the Prophet, long-suffering and merciful to the sins of true believers, who has so purged all believers from evil passions and bad desires, such as embezzlement, bribery, theft, jealousy, weakness and favouritism in every matter, whether appertaining to this world or the next, and has threatened sinners with evil report in this world and torment in the next, and has guided us in the paths of honesty, sincerity, zeal, devotion, obedience, friendliness and faith, and has apportioned a perfect recompense thereto. Next my thanks are due to Her Highness the Ruler of Bhopál, the mighty Shahjahan Begam (may God prosper her fortune!) who, of her grace, appreciation, condescension, and benevolence, which in her are nature's ornaments, first exalted me to the office of Mír Munshí, thereby raising me from the dust to the skies; next of her bounty and liberality selected me and conferred on me the office of Second Minister of State, with all its accessions of rank and estate, and by increasing my rank and dignity invested me with suitable consideration and importance, and gave me the means of showing further loyalty and attachment. It is impossible in these few words to express sufficient thanks for this great appreciation of my services, and it is bad taste for me to speak of my claims to acknowledgment for my own services. Therefore it is now enough for me to promise always to show my heart-felt gratitude for her favours to the best of my powers, and to devote my whole life to further the interests of her issue and of her State. May God increase to me day by day the power to render services to this State by my diligence, zeal, singleness of purpose and devotion! God grant that Her Highness the Ruler (God's blessing be on her!), all her relations and the officers of State may continue satisfied with me to the last day of my life on account of my sincerity, integrity, and open and secret loyalty to the State."

Afterwards, considering the office of Second Minister not good enough for the lofty dignity of this gentleman, I abolished the office from the 1st Safar 1289 A. H.; and, with the sanction of the Government of India, conferred on him the title of Nawáb Wálájáh Amír-ul-Mulk Sayyad Múhammad Siddíḳ Hasan Khạ́n Bahádur. The Nawáb Sáhib, who is a very mine of the jewels of courtesy, and a treasury of true gentility, (may God preserve him!) regarding the commands of the holy writings as absolute, and as the true guide to happiness both in this world and the next, made a settlement of Rs. 25,000 on me in case of separation, and out of his separate maintenance made me an allowance of Rs. 3,000 a year as pin-money.

A noble who receives dignity, rank, and title from his king is proportionately honoured by his contemporaries, is known to the world by that title as long as he lives, and every one in all transactions shows the consideration due to that rank and title. Therefore, on the 24th Zíḳád 1288 A. H., or 4th of February 1872 A. D., I sent an official despatch to Colonel Osborne, C. B., Political Agent, to the following effect:—" When, with the sanction of the Supreme Government, my marriage was contracted with Bakhshí Báḳí Muhammad Khan 'Nasrat Jang,' the following marks of distinction were accorded to him by that Government :—

1st. The title of Nawab with the addition of Nazir-ud-daula.

2nd. A khilat from the Governor-General.

3rd. A salute of 17 guns within the territories of Bhopál.

4th. That he should receive visits from English officers.

5th. That he should receive nazars from the officers of the Bhopál contingent on the occasion of his investiture with the khilat.

6th. That the Assistant to the Political Agent should advance to meet him from the house at Jahángírábád as far as the bridge at the same place.

7th. That the Mír Munshís of the Indore and Sehore Agencies should advance to meet him as far as the Budhwárá Gate.

8th. That the Agent to the Governor-General and the Political Agent of Bhopál should, on the occasion of their presence at Bhopál, visit him at his own house.

These marks of distinction were all accorded by the British Government, while such honours as were the peculiar province of this State, such as the receipt of nazars from all officials, the members of my family, and the officers of State, also the assignment of a suitable estate, were conferred upon him by this Government. Now all the honours granted to my first husband by the British Government and the State ought to be accorded in like manner to Sayyad Siddík Hasam Khan, because by Muhammadan and English law the second husband stands on an equality with the first, and therefore for the husband of the Ruler to be merely a servant of the

State and hold the office of Second Minister is derogatory to the Ruler.

"Thus, there is every reason why Sayyad Siddík Hasan Khan should be raised to the same rank as that enjoyed by the late Nawab Báḳi Muhammd Khan, and it is very important that he should resign the office of Second Minister. Therefore, it is your suppliant's prayer, that the British Government be pleased to grant to Sayyad Siddíḳ Hasan Khan all the honours bestowed on the first Nawab consort, and that the title of "Nawáb Wálájáh Amir-ul-Mulk Sayyad Muhammad Siddíḳ Hasan" be conferred on him. This request was not preferred by me in the first instance, because, although there is divine sanction for the marraige of widows, and the custom is universal among Muhammadans of other countries besides being common in England, yet the Muhammadans of India have abandoned the custom, which is looked upon as strange, and the prejudice of the Hindus against the re-marriage of widows has become firmly rooted in their minds also, although it is contrary to common sense, to the religion of the Muhammadans, and opposed to the English law.

"There are some of my relatives who, from ignorance, disapprove of the marriage of widows; these persons regard with disfavour my second marriage as contrary to the usage of our family, and when they see my second husband advanced to the rank of the first, their rancour will be increased; therefore I deemed it expedient to advance my present husband to the rank of the former by slow degrees. With this end in view, it was in the first place determined to confer upon him the office of Second Minister, which was vacant at the time. Now this office has been abolished, and the income of the estate of the Second Minister, which was allowed every year by the State in my late mother's time, will be absorbed into the State coffers; while an estate equal to that of the late Nawab will be given to my present husband, and his rank will be raised to the same equality. I hope that you will vouchsafe a favourable reply to my plans."

This despatch was translated and forwarded in due course by post, by the Political Agent, to the Agent to the Governor-General for Central India, who, in like manner, forwarded it for the information of His Excellency the Viceroy and Governor-General, who granted my prayer. Afterwards, according to the usual procedure, the despatch, conveying formal sanction, was forwarded to me by the Political Agent on the 17th of December 1872 A. D., or the 18th Rajab 1289 A. H., and on the 10th Shábán he came to Bhopál as the bearer of the khilat, presented by the Governor-General and stayed at the house in Jahángírábád.

On the 11th, the Political Agent proceeded in State with the khilat to the Public Audience Hall in the Palace which had been specially decorated for the occasion. All the officers of State, members of my family, subordinates, and land-owners were assembled, according to custom, and, as usual, a salute was fired, and the appointed ceremony of Istiḳbál was observed. When we had all taken our seats, and the formal greetings had been exchanged, the Political Agent himself placed in my hands the congratulatory despatch, sanctioning the khilat and the title of Nawab, and offered his good wishes, and Munshi Din Diyal, Mir Munshi, by order of the Political Agent, read the despatch aloud from beginning to end, in the presence of the assembly.

This is the purport of the despatch :—

" Before this, on the 17th of September of this year, Your Highness was apprised of the joyful intelligence that the British Government had consented to confer the title of Nawab and a khilat on Nawab Muhammad Siddík Hasan Khan, your beloved husband. Accordingly, to-day it is my pleasing and agreeable duty, in the presence of this joyful assembly, which has been specially convened to witness this auspicious event, to confer on the Nawab the khilat and title which have been bestowed on him by the British Government, and I hereby proclaim before the assembled nobles and officers of the Bhopál State, that the title of Nawab Wálájáh Amir-ul-Mulk, and of a khilat suited to this exalted rank, have been conferred on the Nawab by the British Government, and that that illustrious Government has sanctioned all the marks of distinction appertaining to this rank. It is proper and expedient that the members of the ruling family, the nobles and officers of State, should cordially observe the marks of respect and honour such as former Nawabs of Bhopál enjoyed; and that the Nawab, in gratitude for this splendid boon bestowed on him by the British Government, should endeavour to increase the good reputation of the Ruler, and to advance the interests and prosperity of the people with all his talents and ability.

" It is open to Your Highness and the Nawab to maintain the prosperity and progress of this State, which is already a pattern of good management to other States, and to continue on that path of progress already so well commenced. I now conclude these remarks with this prayer, that the khilat and title may prove a blessing and happiness to Nawab Sayyad Muhammad Siddík Hasan Khan and Your Highness, as well as to all the nobles of this State, and that the attainment of this lofty rank by the Nawab may continue to be a matter of congratulation to Your Highness and to all your family and to the officers of this State. Dated the 15th October 1872."

The Political Agent then invested the Nawab with the khilat, and the Nawab presented a nazar of 101 gold mohurs to the Political Agent, in the name of the Governor-General, and all the ruling family and officers of State and land owners &c., presented nazars to the Nawab according to their respective means. Then the Political Agent took the Nawab with him to the Nawab Kudsia Begam's house, to whom he presented a nazar of one gold mohur and five rupees, on account of her being of greater honour in our family than he, after which the Darbar broke up and the Political Agent returned to his residence.

On this happy occasion, a sum of Rs. 1,000 was presented to the poor out of the State coffers and all public servants contributed seven and a half days' pay to the Nawab, besides the nazars brought in their hands amounting to ten per cent. on their salaries. Although, according to the established custom of the country, fifteen days' pay ought to have been deducted from all officials, the Nawab was good enough to remit seven days' pay, and only to take the other seven days'; one anna out of every rupee of revenue was also allowed by the State, and this sum was to be paid into the public treasury, and to be expended in defraying the cost of a dinner to the poor and to the servants of the State. From the beginning of 1280 Fasli, or the 1st Shaban 1289 A. H., an estate of Rs. 75,472-10-3 was assigned from the State for the use of the Nawab.

The khilat valued at Rs. 10,000, bestowed by the Governor-General, was composed of the following articles:—One diamond aigrette, one large pearl necklace, one turban, one gold embroidered mantle, one shawl, one coat, one piece of kincob, one piece of muslin, one double-barrelled gun, one gold-hilted scimitar, one gold lace sword-belt, one dagger, one bow, one quiver, one shield, one elephant with chaste silver-gilt howdah, with trappings and head-piece, one gold embroidered fan, one velvet-covered throne, one horse with gold and silver trappings and gold embroidered saddle. All these articles the Nawab made over to the State, and received in exchange their money value. After the receipt of the above estate, the Nawab doubled the annual sum of Rs. 3,000, which he had assigned as my allowance, and paid Rs. 6,000 into my private account from the Fasli year 1280."

Her Highness the Begam's anticipations of the beneficial results of this alliance have been fully realized, because ever since her second marriage she has found in her husband an able coadjutor in the administration of the State on whose valuable counsels she may well rely. Out of the numerous measures which have been introduced by the advice of the Nawab Consort for the better administration of the State, I will here note a few of the principal ones, the others will be known on reference to the administration reports of the State:—

1. Efficient police arrangements have been made in the city and the mofussil to afford protection to life and property. The system as obtaining in British territory for the working of the Thuggee and Dacoity Department, has been introduced in the State for the suppression of crime and an extra establishment of police consisting of 45 mounted and 78 foot under three officers entertained, for the arrest of robbers and dacoits. As far as possible the provisions of the Criminal and Civil Procedure Codes have been gradually introduced into the State Courts.

2. The tax hitherto imposed on the ryots in order to meet the expenses attendant on the maintenance of chaukidars, has been abolished, the chaukidars are now being paid from the State revenue, in common with other servants of the State. Municipal dues for lighting the streets and repairing the roads of the city, formerly paid by the subjects, have been abolished, and the expenses are now being met out of the State revenue.

3. In A. D. 1870 the annual contribution of Rs. 12,000 allowed by the State for the repairs of the Hoshangabad and Bhilsa road ceased, since then Rs. 2,65,613-13-6 have been spent on the construction of a new road between Hoshangabad and Bhopál, and in sinking wells and erecting "Dak Bungalows" and "Sarais" on this road for the accommodation of English gentlemen and travellers. An annual allotment of Rs. 13,716 has been made to keep in repairs this new road and an official designated 'Superintendent of

Roads' has been put in charge of it. Careful attention has been directed towards developing the resources of the country by opening up facilities of communication between one district and another.

4. During the life of Her Highness the late Nawab Sikandar Begam the State debts amounted to Rs. 6,78,471-4-6 and 15 gold mohurs, which, by the economical arrangements made by the Nawab Consort, has been liquidated. The long-standing claims of the Solanki jagirdars of Bairasya being left unadjusted during the time of the late Nawab Begam, were finally settled to the satisfaction of all parties concerned; this desirable end was the result of the judicious arrangements made by the Nawab Wálájáh.

5. A new school has been established in the city of Bhopál for the education of the sons of jagirdars and others, the object in view being to qualify them for the duties they may hereafter be called upon to perform. The present cost for the maintenance of this school is Rs. 2,190 annually. Besides this, twenty-eight schools have been established in the mofussil districts for the education of the children of ryots. In these schools Urdu, Nagri and the rudiments of arithmetic are taught. An annual allotment of Rs. 8,165 has been made from the State revenue for the maintenance of these district schools. A new hospital called 'The Prince of Wales Hospital' and a dispensary attached to it have been built at a cost of Rs. 31,494-6 and an annual allotment of Rs. 3,642 has been made for their maintenance. This establishment afforded medical aid to 3,210 patients out of which 28 died. Since March 1871 dispensaries and hospitals have

been established in all the thirty-three parganas, each in charge of a trained *hakím* who is provided with ample medicines &c. The amount sanctioned for the maintenance of these dispensaries is Rs. 20,640. A Vaccine establishment at an annual cost of Rs 6,177-4 has been entertained, which has been the means of saving the lives of many children. The benefit of vaccination is now generally appreciated by the ignorant class who looked upon it with a superstitious dread. From September 1878 to February 1881, 17,692 children were vaccinated.

6. The Bhopál State comprises 3,199 villages, a new land settlement has been made in 2,927 villages after they were surveyed, the revenue of the State has thereby increased.

7. As the proposed scheme for the construction of a Railway line in Bhopál territory was calculated to develop the resources of the country, the proposal was readily assented to by the State. It accordingly agreed to pay a contribution of 50 "lacs" towards the construction of the Railway line. This sum has now been nearly paid up and the Railway is near its completion. Telegraphic communication has already been opened here by a contribution from the State of Rs. 4,000 towards its construction.

7. When war was declared against the Amir of Cabul by the British Government, this State offered to place the Bhopál Battalion at its disposal for service in that country. On the proposal being accepted one hundred carts were furnished by the State for the carriage of the Battalion. On the 8th December 1880 the State contributed Government Rs. 3,000 and the Nawab Consort Rs. 1,000 for the relief of the Euro-

pean and Native soldiers that were wounded in the Afghán war and for the widows and orphans of those that were killed.

On the 3rd February 1880 a contribution of Rs. 1,000 from the State and Rs. 500 from the Nawab Consort was remitted towards the "Daly Memorial School." Both Her Highness the Nawab Shajahan Begam and the Nawab Consort paid their respective quota to the 'Ripon Hospital Fund' at Simla, the Delhi College Fund, the Indore College, the Madras Famine, the 'Eden Hospital,' the Calcutta Zoological Gardens, on their late visit to that place, and the Famine in Ireland.

8. The Bhopál Water Works which was established by Her Highness the late Nawab Kudsia Begam, has been kept up by the State, as also all her charitable and religious endowments, and arrangements have been made to provide for the servants and retainers of Her Highness.

9. By way of an inducement for people to settle down at the new suburb of Shahjahanábád, an advance of Rs. 50,000 has been made to the ryots to enable them to provide themselves with houses. These advances are recovered by small monthly instalments of Rs. 3 per cent., no interest being charged. Out of the money advanced for building purposes 364 houses were built up in the end of 1880 A. D.

10. Orders have been issued to the Civil and Military Departments to afford every means of encouragement for the employment of the Native Christians of Bhopál, according to their fitness in the service of the State, and a provision has been made for the maintenance of their widows and orphans, and for such as have no means of support.

The use of Hindustani words in a book of this kind cannot be avoided. For this reason I have given explanatory notes at the foot of each page in which such words occur, for the enlightenment of those readers that may not be familiar with them.

SAYYAD AKBAR ALAM.

Motimahal, Bhopal,
The 31st August, 1883.

AN INTERPRETER OF WAHABIISM.

PREFACE BY THE AUTHOR.

Reader, I had no need whatever of writing this book, since the long-existing religious discussions among the Indian Musalmans on the tenets of Wahabiism, raged with some vehemence only in the country lying between the waters of the Jamna and the Ganges. No noise of those discussions ever reached the north and the south of India and especially the Native States, the Rulers and the people of which, have always evinced much ignorance on the subject. But for some years past men of all shades of character have begun to pour in from one country into another situated at very long distances and talk of their own views and opinions. But here their designs have to some extent been disclosed. In order to serve their own private ends, they have not hesitated to injure the reputation of simple and straight-forward Mahomedans by means of threats and newly invented appellations in their own tongue.

The subjects of the Bhopal State are mostly Hindus and the remaining few living in the town are Mahomedans, including the foreigners and the natives of the soil. Most of them are illiterate and only a few of them have a smattering of Persian to be serviceable to them in offices and obtaining situations. They are ignorant and negligent of religious controversies; so that no religious question has ever been mooted here by words or writings, and no book or essay has been written by any one to confute the doctrines of any other creed.

The Rulers of Bhopal have ever tried to maintain religious toleration in conformity with the intentions of the Government of India. So that the proverb 'Jesus practises his own religion and Moses his' holds good here in every respect. But for a few years some evil-minded upstarts, protected and patronized by this State, and promoted to exalted positions by my own endeavours, but whose ancestral calling is to injure their own benefactors, have tried to secure their ends by spreading evil reports of Wahabiism against this State and thus excite, against me, the displeasure of the superior authorities. They are intoxicated even yet with their own erroneous ideas. They send anonymous letters to different places through the Post Office and depict newly moulded stories in them, thereby intending to injure me in any way they can. But God defends the truthful from all dangers and sends the liars to perdition either in this world or in the world to come.

On looking at this brewing storm of impudence, and ascertaining the reports I had received about the towns of Upper India, I found out that they were only mediate stratagems used by the informers themselves. The British Government has, in all places and at all times, had an eye to justice in this matter. Never and nowhere has it acted contrary to the facts of a case on mere accusation or false imputation. On the other hand it published a proclamation giving religious freedom to the people and, save the rebels, it never interfered with the religious tenets of either A or B.* It behoves every Government to punish such individuals as foment mischief and disorder and possess all the materials of war and rebellion, be they notorious as Wahabis or not.

He who is ignorant of what his enemies speak against him, such as, calling him a Nedjedi, a Wahabi, or an ir-

---

* The original Urdú has Zaid and Umar, fictitious names employed in exemplifying the rules of Arabic Grammar, cases in law or illustrating certain assertions.

religious person, or otherwise maligning him, is certainly a great friend of his friend, if he has been loyal and his acts untainted with those of enmity and opposition. Experienced men have seen that when a man entertaining feelings of animosity against another man or sect, does not get an opportunity to crush him down, he often seeks to wreak his vengeance under cover of representing him a Wahabi and an enemy of Government. This trick of his now and then succeeds owing to the inexperience of some of the *Hákims** and the imprudence of his helpless opponents. It is only before very discerning judges that all the fraud and mystery of the persecutor are discovered. The British Government is now fully convinced of the fact that the prosecutors in such cases at the time of trial often prove liars and the defendants free from all blame. A rumour bearing upon this view of Government was heard only a short time ago, which the *Pioneer* in its issue dated, Monday, the 8th January 1883, thus corroborates :—

The following resolution, issued by the Government of India, in the Home Department, is published for general information.

"After a careful consideration of all the circumstances of the case, and after consulting the Governments of Bengal and the Panjab, the Governor-General in Council has been pleased to decide that all the Wahabi prisoners, who were sentenced to transportation for life on conviction of the offence of abetting the waging of war against the State, and who are still undergoing their sentence, shall now be released and permitted to return to their homes, conditionally on police surveillance, and subject to such restrictions as to residence as the Local Governments may see fit to prescribe."

Again the *Pioneer* of 11th January, 1883 writes :—

"Quoting the recent Resolution, the *Hindu Patriot* says : 'The Government of India has appropriately opened the

---

* Magistrates or Judges.

new year with this act of grace. Not only the Mahomedans but all classes of our countrymen will hail it with satisfaction. The present Government of India not only knows how to do a right thing, but also to do it at the right moment.'"

A short time before this at the time of the Egyptian war, it was known by a London telegram that Lord Northbrook, a former Governor-General of India, speaking of the Indian Musalmans, said that they were loyal subjects of the British Crown. Accordingly the *Pioneer* dated the 16th October, 1882, published the following intelligence with reference to the speech of the noble Lord, telegraphed from London on the 13th October, 1882 :—

"Lord Northbrook speaking at Liverpool yesterday, expressed great satisfaction at the evidences of sympathy shown by the Musalmans of India with the British policy in Egypt."

What testimony more reliable than this can be had regarding the Mahomedans of India being no enemies of the English Government, be they represented as Wahabis or not. This, no doubt, is really the case.

On the breaking out of the recent war with Egypt, the Bhopal State expressed its readiness to assist the Government with men and money. In reply to this Her Highness the Begam and myself received a letter from Lord Ripon, conveying the thanks of Government for the proffered aid. In the same manner did other Native States of India give proofs of loyalty to the British Government and show marks of great satisfaction on the conquest of Egypt.

The present work has been undertaken with a view to show to Government,

First, That there is no Musalman in the Native States and no British Musalman subject who is inimical to the Supreme Authority ;

Secondly, That such of those living in Native States as have been charged with Wahabiism by their enemies, are certainly no Wahabis ;

Thirdly, How the Masalás* of Jihád† stand in the true religion of Islam; and

Fourthly, That the poor and indigent, as also the wealthy Musalmans that have been before or are still falsely reported against, stand altogether blameless.

Like the Bhopal State but long before it, was Waziruddaula Bahádur, Chief of Tonk, accused of Wahabiism, for no other reason but that he had abolished altogether the mischievous and dangerous rites and customs in his State: such as, grave-worship, worshipping one's spiritual teacher,‡ Táziamaking, &c., &c., But it is known full well how staunch a friend of Government he proved during the Indian Mutiny. Similarly the Bhopal State and its *protegés* be they the descendants of the principal founder of this State, Mian Wazir Mahomed Khan Bahadur, or the servants thereof, whether invested with great or small authority, are all, without exception, well wishers of the British Government. This State stands ahead of all others in this matter. But what can be done with respect to those mischievous spirits who are busy telling whatever they like about you?

This work is also intended to plead in favour of those poor and helpless souls who are causelessly entrapped and who, for ignorance of their religious doctrines, are sometimes severely dealt with on the accusation brought forward by their deadly opponents.

Many persons from Lahore down to Calcutta have, now and then, taken up their pen to write something or other on this topic, according to their respective abilities. But my impression is that the main point of Wahabiism and the orders respecting Jihád in the Islamic faith, have not been propounded with such nicety and minuteness as in the

---

* Precepts of Mahomed.

† A holy or religious war waged by Musalmans against infidels or idolaters.

‡ A representation or model of the tomb of Imám Hasan and Imám Hosain at the anniversary of Moharram.

present volume. Otherwise so many unfounded suspicions occasioned by the innumerable evil reports against one another, in the minds of high English officials, could never have found a place in them, and a sort of freedom from such useless wranglings would have reigned in the minds of both rulers and the ruled.

It will be clear from this book that the charge of Wahabiism against those Musalmans of India who act up to the dictates of the *Korán* and the *Hadís** alone, is utterly wrong and seems to be brought forward out of spite. On the contrary, if at all there is an enemy of the British Government, it must be he who dislikes religious freedom and sticks to the religion, no matter if it be objectionable, of his fathers and forefathers. Or else in India and the Native States in particular, there is no Wahabi in the general acceptation of the word and no atheistical layman and none ill-disposed towards the liberal and benign Government. For it has not been shown who these Wahabis are, where and in what Native States are they to be met with. Nor has it been pointed out what materials of war and rebellion and what means of abetting the rebels they possess. Men evilly disposed try by means of trick and treachery to fasten their own guilt upon others, and thus get themselves honoured by the *Hákims*. But God always puts the liars to disgrace. The discerning *Hákims* immediately discover the truth.

Before writing in this book the translation of my previously compiled works regarding Wahabiism and the *Masálas* of *Jihád*, I wish to add a short introductory chapter on the creation of the world, and the beliefs of the people in it, according to the teachings of Islam and the writings of historians. I purpose also to give the translation of each work in separate chapters and the past events of my life, a narration of which is one main reason for the compilation of

---

* Traditional sayings of the Prophet.

this volume, in the last part of this book, in the hope that Government will justly appreciate my labours.

This treatise proves the innocence of those accused of Wahabiism and attempts to investigate the origin of the term, the bugbear of the English *Hákims ;* as also it serves as an Islamic whip for those ignorant and mischievous persons who call all disorder, wrangling and boxing by the misnomer of jihád.

INTRODUCTION BY THE AUTHOR.

According to the Mahomedans the Creation of the world took place in the following way :—God was in the beginning of all and nothing else. He then created His throne upon water, He then made the Earth and the Firmament. The Throne which is called the *Arsh,* overtops all the heavens like a dome, and cracks like a saddle under the weight of a rider.

He made the Earth on Saturday, Mountains on Sunday, Trees on Monday, Vices on Tuesday, and Light on Wednesday. He spread the animals on this Earth on Thursday. After them all He created Adam, the Progenitor of all mankind, on Friday in the last hours of it, *i. e.,* between the hours of *Asr** and sunset.

The distance between the Earth and the sky (when represented in time) is 500 years. The measure of the thickness of each sky is equivalent to the above distance. All the skies are situated at the space of 500 years from one another. The *Arsh* comes after the seventh heaven. Above this is the Creator of the Heaven and the Earth.

In the same way have the seven Earths been made, each apart from the other by a space of 500 years.

---

* The time of prayer of the Mahomedans before sunset.

The Angels have been made out of light, the genii out of fire, and man has been made out of dust. The stature of Adam was sixty yards in length, the breadth of his body being seven yards. He was the Caliph of God and the first prophet that came to this world. Besides him, it is said, there were one lakh and twenty-four thousand more prophets. But this is a feeble tradition, their number and their books being correctly known to God alone.

God made Adam out of dust collected by handfuls from all places. For this reason some men are white, some black, and some red, according to the colour of the dust. Hence the disposition of every man corresponds with the nature of the dust he is made of: soft, hard, sacred and unsacred dust producing each its own effects.

The sun goes down the *Arsh* in the evening and gets the command of God to rise in the East every morning. On the Doomsday the Almighty will call upon the Sun to rise from where he now sets. From that day fourth no repentance for past sins shall be accepted by God. On that day the Sun and the Moon rolled together shall be thrown into Hell.

Rád* is the name of an angel. The lightning is the whip of fire in his hands. The hot and the cold seasons are the two breaths of Hell.

The Stars are serviceable in three ways. First, they are the ornaments of the sky. Secondly, they are the missiles for Satan. Thirdly, they are the guides on land and sea both by day and night. Besides this all that is said of them as exercising an influence on human destinies, is altogether wrong. A man does not live or die by the rising of a star, nor does he obtain or lose his food by that phenomenon. No danger can approach you, no particle can move from its place, without God's command. He is the only adored One. He is the Master and disposer of all kings on Earth.

---

* The angel of thunder and lightning.

The condition of the followers of *Islám* is like that of water. It is unknown whether the water which precedes is good or that which succeeds it. The loving people are those who have come after (the Prophet) and who, even at the sacrifice of their lives and properties, long to behold the prophet. Some band or other of this people will ever exist in some place or other. The *Hákims* of most countries will be Christians at the approach of the day of the general resurrection.

It appears from the above traditional sayings that although *Islám* will become weaker and weaker every day, still it will not be altogether extinct even to the day of Judgment; that the length and breadth of the Christian dominions will be extensive; and that the Christians will overcome and subdue all. So that the passing events corroborate the above traditions. The attempts therefore of such Musalmans as are unacquainted with the behests of their own religion, to overturn the British Government, and with it destroy the safety and security at present reigning in India, under colour of waging a holy war, are acts of downright stupidity and foolishness. Is it possible that what these rash and inconsiderate people desire can happen, and that the words of the Prophet whose prophecy is now being fulfilled under our own eyes, can be falsified?

However, when God created Adam, He appointed this world to be the first day and the doomsday the next for His descendants. He made the former perishable and the latter everlasting.

Different doctrines prevail with regard to this first day. The Greek, the Persian, the Indian, and the Turkestan philosophers hold that this world has existed from Eternity and will exist to Eternity. Some say that although this world has always existed, it will not last for ever. Mahomedans believe that the world has not always existed and that it will come to an end.

Thus these are the only three views with regard to the existence of the world.

Historians should have dated their histories from the birth of Adam and not from his descent on Earth. They have dropped altogether the interval between the birth and the descent from their calculation. This is as given in the Old Testament.

To cut the story short. Adam alighted on Mount Rahos (?) in Ceylon on Friday the 10th of *Moharram*.* Some say that this paradise the abode of Adam, was above the skies and some maintain that it was on Earth. However, it is not certain where it really was. The tradition goes on to say that Adam died in 930, 1850 years before the Deluge; and that at the time of his death the number of his children had reached to 40,000 souls. The prophets Seth and Enoch were amongst his children.

Noah was born 1640 years after the death of Adam. The Deluge occurred when he was 600 years old. His people were idolaters.

The Deluge lasted six months and ten nights. The Parsees, the Tartars, the Hindus, and the Chinese deny that there was such a flood. The Mahomedans believe the Deluge to have been universal, and, accordingly, call Noah the Second Adam and consider the people of the present age to be his descendants.

Abraham was born 3323 years after Adam and 1081 years after the Flood. People of all denominations believe in him. He died when he was 175 years old, 3498 years after the advent of Adam. He is called the Third Adam.

Ishmael was born when Abraham was 86 years of age and Isaac when he was of 100 years. Joseph was the grandson of Isaac.

Moses was born 425 years after Abraham. At the time of the Exodus he was 80 years of age. He died after reaching the age of 120 years, 3808 years after the descent of Adam.

---

* The name of the first Mahomedan month, held sacred on account of the death of Husain, son of 'Alí, who was killed by Yazíd, near Kufa, in 61 A. H.

Jerusalem was built 529 years after the death of Moses.

Jesus the son of Mary was born on Thursday the 3rd of March, 4 years, 9 months and 9 days before the date from which the Christians reckon their year; and he was raised to the heavens on Friday the 3rd April, in the year 33 of the Christian Era. According to the Christians he was crucified. The Mahomedans say that he was translated to Heaven 5617 years after Adam.

It is now the commencement of 1883 A. D. The Hijra year began on the 16th July 622 A. D. when 2793 years had intervened between Ishmael's settling at Mecca and the journey of our Prophet to Medina. He died on Monday the 12th of *Rabiul Auwal** in the 11th year of the Hijra, which corresponds to 8th June 632 A. D. According to the Christians 7704 years have elapsed since the time of Adam, up to the present year 1300 A. H. or 1883 A. D.

For 30 years after the death of our Prophet his people followed the same course of conduct as they had done during his life-time. Then kingdoms were established and times were changed.

There were 14 kings of the house of Omayya. Their reign was put an end to in the year 132 A. H. They were followed by 37 kings of the Abbiside Dynasty. Their reign commenced on Friday the 13th *Rabiul Auwal* in the year 132 A. H.; and ended on 6th *Safar*† 656 A. H. They reigned for a period of about 520 years and 2 months.

In the year 371 A. D., Islam was brought into India by Nasiruddin, the king of Gazni. After this occurred the twelve expeditions of Mahmud of Gazni to India. He was a Satrap of the Caliph of Bagdád. In his time the Mahomedan conquests extended to Kanauj. His last expedition to India was in the year 1024 A. D. Since that year the Mahomedan rule began to extend. In the year 1150 A. H.

---

* The third Mahomedan month. † The second Mahomedan month.

the English gained some footing at Murshidábád, and their power began to increase.

Her Majesty Queen Victoria, now Empress of India, ascended the throne in the year 1254 A. H.

Full particulars regarding the provinces of India and the different battles fought in it, up to the year 1197 A. H. are given in *Sairul-Motaakherin*.

This country is now under the complete subjugation of Britain. Everything is done according to the wishes of the authorities; and this rule has been observed under all Governments of whatever religious persuasions, and is nothing new. It is clear from the perusal of the histories of past times that the protection, ease, and liberty which the people in general enjoy under the auspices of the British rule, were not to be met with under any other power. And no doubt they are the result of the religious freedom that the English have bestowed on the people of all denominations. In a word we may refer to the proclamation of 1st January, 1877 A. D., read with so much pomp and ceremony to all the Chiefs and Nobles assembled at the Delhí Darbár, on the occasion of the assumption, by Her Majesty, of the title of the Empress of India. This proclamation was printed and published in Urdu and circulated throughout India. In the course of his long speech delivered on the occasion, the Viceroy said: "Now, under laws which impartially protect all races and all creeds, every subject of Her Majesty may peacefully enjoy his own. The toleration of the Government permits each member of the community to follow without molestation the rules and rites of his religion. The strong hand of Imperial Power is put forth, not to crush but to protect and guide; and the results of British rule are everywhere around us in the rapid advance of the whole country and the increasing prosperity of all its Provinces."

After separately addressing the British administrators and the members of the Civil and Military services, the Viceroy drew the attention of the Princes and people of India to the words of the gracious message telegraphed by Her Majesty on the occasion, remarking in the end of his speech that he felt confident, they would appreciate the words. The words of the telegraphic message are:—

"We, Victoria By The Grace Of God, of the United Kingdom, Queen, Empress Of India, send through our Viceroy to all our Officers, Civil and Military, and to all Princes, Chiefs and peoples, now at Delhi assembled, our Royal and Imperial Greeting, and assure them of the deep interest and earnest affection with which we regard the people of our Indian Empire. We have witnessed with heartfelt satisfaction the reception which they have accorded to our beloved Son, and have been touched by the evidence of their loyalty and attachment to our House and Throne. We trust that the present occasion may tend to unite in bonds of yet closer affection Ourselves and our subjects ; that from the highest to the humblest all may feel that under Our rule the great principles of liberty, equity and justice, are secured to them and that to promote their happiness, to add to their prosperity, and advance their welfare, are the ever present aims and objects of Our Empire."

This proclamation on behalf of the Queen-Empress of India read to the Delhi Assemblage by Lord Lytton, her representative and Viceroy of India, and then published, demands our highest esteem. It is a great charter of liberty for the people of India in general and the Native Chiefs and Princes in particular. It resembles the treaties entered into with Native States. It is a safe-guard against the high-handed proceedings of *Hákims* and the evil machinations of mischief-mongers, should they take it into their heads to harass and persecute the innocent people, rich or poor.

CHAPTER I.

This Chapter contains a reproduction in Urdú from *Hidáyatus sáil ela Adala-tul-Masail*. This book was compiled in 1291 A. H., ten years ago, and was published in 1292 A. H. It is devoted to questions and answers with respect to prayers and fasts. A certain person has put a question in that book, a translation and my answer to it I subjoin below. The reason why I do so is this: My connection with Bhopal extends over a period of thirty years. During this period I have lived always respected. Never did I hear the epithet 'Wahabi' applied to either the late Nawáb Sikandar Bégam, Her Highness the present ruler of Bhópal, myself or any other servant of this State. But at the time of the rupture with the late Nawáb Qudsia Bégam,* some of the upstarts and servants of this State that were really *Shias* and declared themselves to be *Sunnis*, having combined with the intriguing and seditious servants of the Bégam, accused this State and myself of Wahabiism and took this unfounded charge to the ear of the Authorities. To expose the falsehood of this malicious accusation it is necessary to reproduce here what I wrote respecting Wahabiism many years before this charge was laid to my door, when the enemies of this State had not even the remotest thought of their calumnious after-doings.

Question. Who was Abdul Wahab of Nedjed, the so-called founder of the Wahabis? Did his religious tenets correspond with those of the *Sunnis*, or not?

Answer. Those who say that Abdul Wahab was the founder of the Wahabi sect, are evidently in the wrong. Inasmuch

---

* Mother of Nawáb Sikandar Bégam and grandmother of the present ruler of Bhopal, Nawáb Sháh Jahán Bégam, G.C.S.I. She was born in 1801 and died in 1882.

as it was Mahomed his son and not he that invited the people of his country to embrace his religious views, *i. e.*, the tenets of Imám Hambal. Abdul Wahab was not the founder of any new religious denomination. Both he and his son were the followers of the above Imam. While the Indian Musalmans are either *Shias*, and the followers of Imam Abū Hanifa, or *Ámil-bil-Hadís*, *i. e.*, htose who follow the sayings of the Prophet without reference to any particular *Imám*. The followers of Imám Hambal are not to be found in India.

Mahomed, the son of Abdul Wahab, was born in Ainia in the Province of Nedjed, in the year 1115 A. H, In 1200 A. H. he made himself public in parts of Hedjás and Yaman. He died in 1206 A. H. and belonged to the *Hambli*[*] church. The followers of Imam Hambal are generally found in Hedjás and Yaman.

True *Islám* enjoins adherence to the Korán and the sayings of the Prophet, and not to the teachings of any particular professor of religion. It is therefore evidently wrong to call Abdul Wahab and his son, who lived and died as *Hamblis*, founders of any new religious sect. To charge therefore such Musalmans as act up to the dictates of the *Korán* and follow the sayings of the Prophet alone, with being the followers and apostles of Abdul Wahab, betrays sheer ignorance and a spirit of uncharitableness.

An orthodox Musalman thinks it his first duty to obey God and His Prophet in the face of all other religious and sectarian views. He makes God and His Prophet his sole guide and pays no regard to the words of any religious dema-

---

[*] The Mahomedan religion is divided into four principal sects or churches. The *Hanafis* follow Imam Abú Hanifa; the *Shafais* have for their spiritual leader Imám Shafai; the *Malikis* have Imam Malik; and the *Hamblis* have Imam Hambal for their spiritual head. The *Ahl-e-Hadis* or the *Ahl-e-Sunnat* and *Jamqat*, are those who follow the Korán and the Hadis alone and do not conform themselves to the teaching of any of the four sects mentioned above.

gogues, not to mention Mahomed *bin** Abdul Wahab who is of no consequence compared to them. *Islám* has produced thousands of learned men, but no Musalman, even the very lowest, thinks it his duty to tread in their path or believes that he will arrive at the real truth only by adopting any particular course indicated by them.

The history of the Musalmans of India when mentioned in connection with this subject is briefly this:—With the introduction and propogation of *Islám* in India the rulers of this country happened by chance to be *Hanafis*. The people as a rule followed them. This state of things once commenced has continued up to this time. As a matter of course, all the learned men, *Ḳazis*, *Muftis*, and other State officials and influential persons, were men of the *Hanafia* persuasion. So that a body of learned men collected *Fatwae*† *Hindia*, called also *Fatwáe Alamgiri* for having been compiled by the order and during the reign of the Emperor Aurangzebe, Alamgir. Sheikh Abdurrahím of Delhi, father of the well-known Shah Walíulláh, was also among the number.

After him came Shah Walíullah a great *Mohaddis*‡ and doctor among the *Hanafis* and a strict adherent of *Sunnat* and *Jamáat*. He examined good many religious doctrines then prevalent and distinguished between the sound and the unsound ones.

Mahomed Ismáíl of Delhi, his grandson, followed in his wake. He explained the true laws of Mahomed and rooted out paganistic theories and heretical doctrines which greatly interfere with the peace and well-being of Musalmans in this as well as the next world. He eradicated many evils and customs that were productive of mischief in this and the world to come. It was owing to his teachings that

---

* Son of.

† Orders or sentences of Ḳazis under the Mahomedan rule in India.

‡ One versed in Hadises or the sayings of the Prophet.

many of the Indian Musalmans left *tázia*-worship, *nautch** parties, and other evil habits and immoral customs. It was he who impressed upon their minds that to cherish a spirit of disloyalty towards the reigning power, was an unpardonable sin in the eyes of both God and man; and turned the attention of the people towards the true sayings and the invaluable precepts of the Prophet. Schools and mosques sprung up as the result of his pious labours. Places of ill-repute, such as *Bhangérkhúná*,† *Madak-khánâ*‡ liquor-shops, and brothels, ceased to exist. These places the haunts of the *badmáshes*§ and vagabonds of the land, who were the source of constant uneasiness to Government, no more existing, the country settled into tranquillity. In none of Maulvi Ismáíl's works is there any mention of the doctrine of *Jihád*, not to speak of *Jihád* with the British Government which rather recognized and appreciated his services. This fact is proved by the writings of Syed Ahmad Khan, C. S. I. Notwithstanding the intrigues of many evil-minded and mischievous persons, the British Government did not pay any heed to the false accusations brought forward by them against the Maulvie, nor did it in any way interfere with him.

In short the family of Mahomed bin Abdul Wahab was the follower of the tenets of Imám Hambal and that Maulvi Mahomed Ismáil, a native of India, had no connection with him as a disciple. Nor is there any reason to suppose that they were known to each other. How then are the learned

---

* Dancing which is prohibited in Islám.

† A shop or house where those addicted to the use of *bháng* assemble. The leaves of the *bhang* plant (*Cannabis sativus*) are first well-pounded in a stone or iron mortar and then mixed with water, sugar and other ingredients, are taken as an exhilarating drink by the high caste Hindus who refrain from intoxicating drinks.

‡ A place where pellets of opium are smoked. Nowadays such places are numerous and Mahomedans generally resort to them.

§ Disreputable persons. Bad characters.

and the illiterate of this country, spoken of as followers of Mahomed *bin* Abdul Waháb, is a mystery to every thinking mind, and betrays nothing but sheer ignorance and inimical feelings of a certain class of people. For everybody knows that since the time of Mahomed *bin* Abdul Waháb up to the present, there has been no communication or friendly intercourse between the people of India and the inhabitants of Nedjed. The Arabian Seâ separates them, and they live at a distance of thousands of miles from one another. Both in their worldly pursuits and the observance of their religion, you will find that what obtains here is unheard of in that country and *vice versâ*. In short there is not the least comparison between the ways and manners of the people of this country and those of the Nedjedians. Moreover none of the sects of the Indian Musalmans has even maintained, in words or writings, that true faith and pure *Islám* are to be found in the followers of the Nedjedian teachers alone, and that the rest are only a benighted flock. Every right-thinking man can find out for himself whether it is a fact.

Many works in Arabic, Persian, and Urdu of all sizes, written by the scholars of Delhi, do exist to this day, and I challenge any one to point out in them anything contrary to what I have said above.

In a word not to follow the teachings of any particular person but the behests of the *Korán* and the sayings of the Prophet, that forbid acts calculated to disturb the public peace, is the main principle of the Islamic faith. This is true as regards the learned men of all parts of the Mahomedan world, be they of Nedjed, of Upper India, Sindh or the Deccan.

We are neither the followers of Mahomed *bin* Abdul Waháb of Nedjed nor of Mahomed Ismáil. The *Korán* and the *Hadis* are our guide. We regard all learned men in the same light. We do not follow or fight for the religious doctrines of any one of them in particular, it being altogether against the teachings of *Islám* to do so.

Let us now briefly glance over Wahabiism and the different shapes it has assumed in different parts of India. Our ignorant Mahomedan brethren of India everywhere attach a different signification to the word Wahabiism. In the country between the Jamna and the Ganges, the term *Wahábi* signifies one who preaches against grave and *tázia* worship, the asking of help from saints, and attending *majlis-e-Maulúd*, and prevents people saying ' *Ya Rasul ullah*'* and ' *Ya Ali*.'†

In Hydrábad and the Deccan, the word *wahábí* denotes a person who refrains from drinking toddy, keeps his *paejámá*‡ above his ankle, does not shave his beard and observes prayers and fasts.

In Bombay a *Wahábí* is one who does not regard Sheikh Abdul Qádir of Gilán, a man noted for learning and piety and a follower of Imam Hambal, as master of the world, and looks upon *Majlis-e-Maulúd*§ as a heretical innovation.

A *Wahábí* in Bengal is one who does not follow or abide by the rules of any of the four churches of *Islám*, but walks by the true and safe path indicated by the Prophet and keeps himself aloof from those religious innovations, the product of the reasoning of certain minds, sprung up after the death of the Prophet.

With some a *Wahábí* is one who combines in himself the attributes above stated. In India the term *Wahabiism* is generally used in contradistinction to *Bidat.*‖ The *bidatis* are men who stick to those religious views and rites that

---

* O Prophet of God!

† O Ali! Ali was Mahomed's son-in-law. He was, according to the *Sunnis*, the fourth *Khalifa* or successor of Mahomed, but the *Shias* make him the direct successor, not acknowledging the other three Caliphs.

‡ A loose garment worn generally by Mahomedans extending from the waist to the ankle, and covering the lower limbs. Trousers.

§ A religious assembly to celebrate the birth-day of the Prophet.

‖ Heresy in religion, such as worshipping the dead, making *tazias*, offering sweetmeats to dead relations, &c., &c.

have sprung up after the time of the Prophet; who maintain that it is not right and proper to be guided by his sayings and personal examples; who adore *fakirs** and derveshes, bow down to them and make them vows and oblations; and who practise *chillás*† at religious shrines, offering up sweetmeats of various kinds. They look upon the souls of derveshes as ruling and pervading the whole system of the universe and as minutely acquainted with the things of the invisible world. Bad customs, meaningless ceremonies and pagan doctrines prevail in such people. As a proof of their deceit and falsehood, it may be mentioned that they have impressed upon the minds of the present English rulers that the Wahábís as a class are their enemies, that they intend to kill them, and destroy the existing Government, and that they seriously intend disturbing the peace and well-being of the people of India. On the other hand, supposing the Wahábís to be really such as they have been represented, still no sensible and wise man will be able to prove the truth of the accusation that they entertain serious thoughts against the existing order of things. India will in that case be a *darul-harb*‡ and not a *dárul-Islám*;§ and to live in a *darul-harb* under the Government of a people professing a different religion from that of *Islám*, with the enjoyment of perfect peace, does not authorize any Mahomedan to entertain even thoughts of *Jihád*.

In the year of the Mutiny some of the turbulent and mischievous souls among the ignorant and illiterate populace, who raised a cry of *Jihád*, beat and oppressed women and

---

* Men who lead what is called a holy life.

† Forty days spent at a religious shrine in worship and all sorts of privations.

‡ Literally, the mansion of war. A country where the Musalman religion does not prevail.

§ A country where Islám prevails and where every Mahomedan can perform his religious rites or ceremonies without let or hindrance.

children, and pillaged and plundered the wealth and properties of the ryots, were shamefully wrong and evidently guilty of a great crime. Because according to the *Korán* and the *Hadís* none of the conditions that make *jihád* imperative, existed at that time. Nothing but madness, stupid imagination and a desire of sovereignty and conquest, could have entered their heads and souls. Only God knows whether any of the rebellious populace and the mutinous sepoys possessed in them purity of purpose, chastity of intention, love of justice and a true spirit of *Islám*.

In conclusion those who have been dubbed Wahábís by their enemies in India, are not, in my opinion and that of experienced men, Wahábís. To characterize such persons as follow the *Korán* and the *Hadís*, observe prayers and fasts and other religious behests just according to the laws of *Islam*, by the name of Wahábís, is surely great injustice and cruelty. The *Korán* and the *Hadís* do not oblige any Mahomedan to rebel against the ruler, for the time being, of his country, or disturb the peace of mankind and stand in the way of the public good. They do rather prohibit such a course of procedure.

Now remains the consideration of the question of *Jihád* against non-Moslems. Its excellence is to be found narrated in the religious laws of the Mahomedans of all sects and schisms, *bidati*, *Sunni*, *Shia*, *Rafzi*,* *Kharji*,† &c, &c. ; and all of them agree in believing *Jihád* to be imperative only when all the causes and conditions for it exist. No Mahomedan can deny this. But the mere existence of an injunction in our *Shariat*‡ does not render its performance obligatory. This neither reason nor our *Shariat* dictates.

---

* A heretic, particurlarly a *Shia*.

† Literally, one who has been excluded. A sect of Mahomedans who do not reckon 'Alí among the legal successors of the Prophet : they are the mortal enemies of the *Ráfzis* or *Shias*, who reject Abú Bakr, 'Umar, and Usmán, while Sunnis consider the four as legal successors.

‡ The laws of Mahomed.

It is quite manifest and known to all the historians that no Nedjedian in the garb of a learned teacher has come to India, who has converted the people and propagated his religious tenets all over the Indian towns and villages, and who has acquired any footing or authority sufficiently alluring for the people to follow his footsteps and 'sing his song.' Neither does any relationship like that between a religious teacher and his disciple, exist between the Nedjedians and the Indians, which can justify us in saying that the latter are the followers of the former. Nor do the Indians possess any means of communication, such as newspapers, Railways and Telegraphs, with the Nedjedians, as is possessed by them with the English, the French or the Germans, as to lead us to the above conclusion. In short to connect the Indian Musalmans with the Wahabis of Nedjed, is sheer ignorance, downright foolishness, and a palpable mistake.

To report against the so-called Wáhabís of India and lay unfounded charges at their door, when they object to the very appellation, and then feed one's private grudge, is surely highly unjust. At the present day the Nedjedian Arabs frequent the port of Bombay for trade and the *Hakims*, fully aware of the fact, do not at all interfere with their business; because the British Government deals out punishment to the rebellious and the seditious only and has nothing to do with A or B.

The *Hadis* reported by Abdullah *bin* Umar contains the following sayings of the Prophet:—"The Israelites have split up into seventy-two tribes and my people shall be divided into seventy-three. All of these shall be thrown into fire except one sect." One of his (Mahomed's) companions asked which that one sect was. He replied "that sect which follows my religion and that of my companions." In *Tirmizi* occurs the following with reference to this *Hadis*:—"Seventy-two sects of my people shall go into

Hell and one into Heaven; and that the name of this sect shall be *Jamaat*. Ere long some sects will spring up from my people, in whom heresy will penetrate in the same manner as disease penetrates into the body of one by dog-bite. No vein or joint will be safe from this heretical distemper. It will creep into them."

It appears from the above quoted *Hadis* that those who act up to the dictates of the *Korán* and the *Hadis*, are called *Sunnis* and not *Wáhabís*. The Indian Musalmans are mostly *Sunnis* and not *Hamblis*.

In the works written by learned Mahomedan divines where the above alluded seventy-two sects have been enumerated name by name, there is no mention whatever of the name Wahábí. It also appears from the above-mentioned *Hadis* that any one originating a new sect or doctrine or inventing a new religion or seditious tenets, from the ancient *Islam*, is a heretic and an idealist and doomed for Hell. Now then how can a true Mahomedan follow a newly set up doctrine, and like to be known by a newly invented appellation?

CHAPTER II.

In *Mawaidul Awaid* is to be found a mention of the necessary *Hadises*, and the invaluable benefits resulting from them. The following is an extract from the contents of the 33rd page of that book :—

Abi Horaira relates that Mahomed (may the mercy of God be upon him and his posterity) said "Those who believe in God and his Prophet, and are incessant in their daily prayers and unfailing in the performance of the Fast of *Ramzan**, for the sake of virtue and benevolence alone, shall have paradise for their abode, whether they wage war against infidels or remain where they were born. Therefore, when you desire for anything from God, ask for *Jannat-ul-Firdaus*, because it is the centre of all the heavens, higher than all of them, has the seat of the Merciful upon it, and is the source of the different streams of heaven."

It is manifest from the above *Hadis* that *Jihád* against the opponents of Islam is a *farz-kefaya*, i. e., if the people of one country wage a religious war, it is not incumbent upon the people of another to do the same. *Jihád* is not imperative upon every individual Musalman in the shape of a command which, if not obeyed, would hurt his Islamic faith. True faith and *Islam* are sufficient guarantees for one to enter paradise, even if he do not stir abroad to wage religious wars against the infidels all the days of his life. This the majority of Mahomedan doctors agree in asserting.

Now as regards the virtues and the excellence of *Jihád*, the *Korán* and other religious works are filled with their enumeration. A translation thereof is to be found in all

---

* The name of the ninth Mahomedan month, during which the Mahomedans are interdicted from eating, drinking, and conjugal duty between the morning dawn and the appearance of the stars at eventide.

the Mahomedan world. The original Arabic and the translations of it in Urdu and Persian are equally read by the young and old, men and women, in all towns and villages. I doubt whether there is any village or town which does not possess such works. But the reward and recompense of this can be obtained only when all the causes and conditions for undertaking a *jihád* exist according to the *Shara*.*

The Mahomedan public, now-a-days, for the most part possessing no sense or learning, and more prominently those endowed with wealth and authority among them, have misunderstood sedition for *jihád*. No one possessing an iota of sense and learning can support or acknowledge their misguided zeal. Accordingly in the year of the Mutiny some of the Indian Rajas, Babus, Nawabs, and Nobles, made India the hot-bed of disorder, strife and commotion, in the name of *jihád*. This spirit of revolt and open resistance raged so high in them that even women and children whom every *Shariat* protects from massacre, were made the innocent victims of their bloody swords. Now this act of theirs is regarded by every Mahomedan as quite opposed to the laws of Mahomed and is never justifiable in any sect of *Islám*. Any one fomenting such a sedition at the present day is from beginning to end vicious and is a slanderer of *Islám*.

The Mahomedan theologians are not at one with regard to the proposition whether India is a *dár-ul-harb* or a *dár-ul Islám* since the advent of the English rule. Those of the *Hanafia* church, to which the Indian Musalmans mostly belong unanimously assert that India is a *dar-ul-Islám*. When India is so regarded, *jihád* can have no meaning here.

Again, to wage religious wars against the very rulers under the shadow of whose benign government we live in the perfect enjoyment of peace, is highly sinful even with such Mahomedan doctors, inclusive of some of those at Delhi,

---

* The precepts of Mahomed.

who say that this country is a *dár-ul-harb;* as long as we do not abandon the country and settle in another where *Islám* prevails.

In fine, to live in a *dár-ul-harb* and wage *jihád* in it, is on no account justifiable either in the eyes of the ancient or the modern Musalmans.

The principal condition for waging *jihád* is to be the follower of such an *Imám** as combines in himself wisdom, learning, justice, acuteness of intellect, and a penetrating judgment and possesses all the attributes of a spiritual guide. The wise, sensible, and experienced portion of the population must approve of his *Imámat*† and make him, with full consent and wish, without external force or aversion, their temporal and spiritual head. The women and the children, the old and the infirm, must not be put to death. If any person other than the true *Imám* claim his office, he must be put to the sword as rebellious.

The above conditions were all absent during the mutiny. On the other hand whoever had a temptation of authority instilled into him, raised, in every town and village, a standard of revolt and delighted in calling the tumult by the name of *jihád*. Whereas it was no *jihád* at all but an unqualified sedition.

In short to think of waging *jihád* in India at the present day when peace with religious freedom in accordance with the proclamation of Government at the Delhi Darbar, is the order of the day, on the basis of the Mahomedan laws, is nothing but madness. And he that, like King Noodle, unnecessarily commits riot and assault, and spreads plunder and rapine, under the plea of *jihád*, is acting wholly against his religious laws and, instead of gaining anything by destroying the lives and properties of his fellow beings, loses his own honour and respectability. The principle is that no act can be rewarded in the future unless that act is done

---

* A spiritual head or leader.

† Spiritual leadership.

only for the sake of God and is in accordance with the laws of our religion; and so long as these conditions are not fulfilled the lives and properties destroyed in the performance of the act are regarded as lost in this world and in the world to come.

I wonder at those persons who, during the mutiny sanctified the anarchy, the alarm, and the gathering set up by the ignorant and the mischievous, by the name of *jihád*, when no cause existed for it, when no *Imám* appeared on the field, when innocent women and children were not spared, and which our religion did not at all authorize. It is unknown what *Korán* gave them the above command and what *Hadis* the proof for it. What makes the matter worse is, that at the time of the mutiny, most of the leaders were Rajas and Hindu chiefs whose spiritual leadership is entirely forbidden in all sects of *Islám*. The people who then rebelled against the British Government, were also mostly Hindus whose alliance, offensive or defensive, in *jihád* our *Hadis* clearly prohibits. But even granting that they had nothing but *Islám* on their lips, still to talk of *jihád* is sheer nonsense, as long as we do not leave the country that is a *dár-ul-harb* for one that is a *dár-ul-Islám*, to settle therein, and do not appoint a man possessing all the qualifications of an *Imam*, as our spiritual and temporal guide. But a person answering all the conditions of an *Imám* is as rare in these days as one possessing a knowledge of alchemy and the phœnix. So much so that even among the Mahomedan rulers and governors of the present day there is not one individual who is possessed of the necessary attributes of an *Imám*, or is acquainted with the forms and etiquette, the ways and means of sovereignty and power, the rebels and the mutineers being out of the question.

It is this reason that most of the doctors of *Islám* have not regarded the wars waged by Tamerlane, Akbar and other Emperors, as *jihád*, because their battles that disturbed the tranquil state of the country, were undertaken for conquest and sovereignty

Imám Shaukání in his work called *Badar Tálá*, speaking of Tamerlane says that Tamerlane once asked the doctors of his Court whether his or his enemies' men that were slain in battles, were to enter heaven? One of them replied:— "Mahomed (may the peace of God be upon him and his posterity) has said—some fight for zeal, some for the display of valour, and some for the exhibition of skill in war. Of these, only those are destined for heaven who fight for God only."

In short the true object of *jihád* is to exalt the word of God and establish peace and security in His Kingdom. Desire of conquest, reputation and renown, should never be the object in view. Such battles, therefore, as have been fought for conquest, sovereignty and power, are thousands of miles away from the *jihád* of our *Shara*, and those that fight such battles can never be counted in the category of *mojáhids*.* For this reason *Ibn* Arab Sháh in his work called *Ajáebul Makdúr* and Sewti in his *Tarikh-ul-Khúlafa*, have satirized Tamerlane and condemned him for his having called his battles *jihád*.

All the Mahomedan doctors agree in saying that the commands in our *Shariat* have reference to the spirit and not to the name of a thing. By altering the name we do not change the nature of it. As for instance, *súd*† does not become a lawful gain by changing its name to *munáfa*‡. Imám Shaukání in *Fatah Rabbani*, an Arabic work of his, writes to the same effect; and in his book, called *Tambíh-ul-Amsál*, declares that the battles fought by kings for wealth and dominion were no *jihád*. The following is the substance of what he writes on this subject:—

---

* Warriors in the defence of the true faith.
† Interest on loans that the Mahomedans are forbidden to take.
‡ Lawful profits of trade.

"Those kings who, notwithstanding the commands of their religion to the contrary, take the wealth of their subjects, with or without their will, to carry on wars, instead of benefitting cause them great loss. As for instance, the wars carried on by some kings, by which every one of them wished to secure the sovereignty for himself, were nothing but the result of ignorance and foolishness. It often happens in these wars that the soldiers and sepoys dishonour and kill the weak and the old, and plunder their wealth and properties. How great is this oppression!"

Now it is manifest from the above that the battles fought during the mutiny were no *jihád*. And how can they be so regarded, when we consider, how greatly they interfered with the safety and security, the quiet and repose, of the people, established by the British rule in India. The ryots could not obtain service for want of confidence in themselves. The safety of their life, property and honour, existed only in their fancy.

Where Imám Shaukání* (may the mercy of God be upon him) treats of the justice of rulers in general, he writes this also:—"If justice cannot be done according to the laws of *Islám*, we must imitate the English rulers in attending to the welfare of the subjects and the redress of their grievances."

It is evident from the above testimony that no nation can compare with the English at the present day in the improvement of their country, the peace, the protection and the happiness of the people they have effected and established. Although *Mollás*† and *Muftis*‡ have, out of flattery, written and talked much in the praise of everybody, yet I have stated only as much as appeared to me good and true; acceptance and guidance are in the hand of God.

---

* He was a *Kazi* of Shaukán in Yaman and an *Ahle-Hadis*.

† A Mahomedan lawyer, doctor or schoolmaster.

‡ A Mahomedan lawgiver.

CHAPTER III.

In page 36 of Mawaid-ul-Awaid is an account to the following purport:—It is related by Ibn Umar that when Mahomed invoked the blessing of God upon Syria and Yaman, his men requested him to do the same for Nedjed. The narrator says he imagines that Mahomed, when asked for the third time by his men to pray for Nedjed, replied—"Tumult and sedition shall rise from there and the horn of Satan protrude from the selfsame spot."

In India the worshippers of tombs and adorers of saints have, out of sheer enmity and illwill, nicknamed the believers of one true God Wahábis, in the notion that the latter are connected with Mahomed *bin* Abdul Waháb of Nedjed. They denounce that country on the authority of the above-mentioned *Hadis,* and argue that when *Bin* Abdul Waháb, a native of the place, has been a bad man his followers must also be bad. We had better drop this argument, it has no connection with India but with a foreign country.

To call the believers of one Supreme and Omnipotent Deity by the name of Wahábis and connect them with Mahomed *bin* Abdul Waháb is a mistake and a lie for various reasons :

First. They do not call themselves by that name; nor do they derive their origin from Abdul Waháb. They have not selected for themselves the name they go by, unlike *Shias* who have chosen to call themselves such in contradistinction to *Sunnis.* Had they chosen the name 'Wahábis' for themselves they would have evidenced something indicated by the term. On the other hand they hate the appellation and deny any connection with the title. It is certainly illegal and unreasonable therefore to call any one by an annoying title or nickname. The truth is that we, the believers of one God and followers of the one true prophet, consider it an abuse to be called Wahábis, and do not connect ourselves with any of the ancient famous *Imáms*. Neither do we call ourselves *Hanafis* or *Shafais*, nor are we pleased with the title *Hamblis* or *Málikís*. How is it possible then to follow Mahomed *bin* Abdul Waháb and accept the creed set up by him?

Secondly. In order to be initiated into the secrets of any religion, it is necessary that one should be the pupil of a religious teacher, or be his home disciple, believe in his powers or be his fellow countryman.—Now then, the admission of the Indian Musalmans into the creed of Abdul Waháb, depends upon their passing through the above initiatory stages. But it so happens that they do not possess any of the connecting links to favour the above presumption. In the face of these circumstances, it is a great mistake, therefore, to connect the Mahomedans of India with Mahomed *bin* Abdul Waháb of Nedjed.

Thirdly. A long period has elapsed since the death of Mahomed *bin* Abdul Waháb. In Nedjed where he was born and bred, he has not left any of his grandsons or great-grandsons to teach his doctrine to the people or persuade the Indians and the Arabians to settle in that country. Nor do the Indians follow his creed or conform themselves to his teachings. It is highly against justice and equity then to call them Wahábis and connect them with Mahomed *bin* Abdul Waháb.

Fourthly. Conversion into any religion or religious denomination, is also effected by reading and hearing about it and mixing with men professing that religion. For instance, owing to free intercourse of the Indian Musalmans with the Hindus, many of the prevalent customs of the latter have been adopted by the former and observed by them in weddings and nuptials for many years. It is a well-known fact that no work of Mahomed *bin* Abdul Waháb has been published in India that is read in *Madrasas** or circulated

---

* Schools for the diffusion of Mahomedan learning.

among the Mahomedan doctors for perusal. He himself belonged to the *Hambli* church, as most of the people of Nedjed where he was born, are *Hamblis*. In the same way most of the Musalmans of India belong to the *Hanafia* creed. Mahomed *bin* Abdul Waháb was not the founder of any new religion the followers of which can be called Wahábis. If he did originate any new religion, no book dealing with it is extant in this country, though it may be found in his. We who worship one God and follow the course shown by our Prophet, do not like to imitate the teachings of the *Hanafia*, the *Sháfai*, the *Málikí*, or the *Hambli* creed. For this reason the charge of Wahábiism can never be preferred against us with propriety and justice. The religious doctrines of the worshippers of one God are these :—To pray at stated times and to observe the Fast. To do our duties with respect to our parents and relations. To conform to the rites and ceremonies prescribed in the *Shara*, at the time of marriages and funerals; and to refrain from noise, nautch and revelry. To obey the command of God and His Prophet and of no one else, whether it be on the subject of *jihád* or any other religious topics. How cruel, therefore, is it to nickname such as follow the above principles Wahábis!

Fifthly. There has been no communication between the inhabitants of India and those of Nedjed. Neither is there any place of worship like *Kábá** in Arabia, where the Indians cannot but resort to, and there imbibe the religion of Mahomed *bin* Abdul Waháb and on return propagate it in their own country. Nor is it the seat of any flourishing trade where they can go for buying the articles of commerce and thereby contract the religious notions of that country and inaugurate them in their own. They possess no epistolary communications with the people of Nedjed by which the Indian Musalmans can have imitated their ideas of religion. To establish, therefore, a relation, notwith-

---

* The temple of Mecca.

standing the non-existence of it, with Mahomed *bin* Abdul Waháb and the Mahomedans of this country is a strange sort of calumny. It is worthy of great consideration that we look upon the ordinances of God and our Prophet as our sole guides in life, and do not choose to be reckoned among the followers of the great ancient doctors of law and religion. How then is it possible to be highly pleased with the declaration of our connection with Mahomed *bin* Abdul Waháb, when he himself belonged to a separate religion called Hambli? This freedom of ours from the prevalent religious forms of the modern times, are no doubt, the intention of the English laws and not that of bigotry and superstition. It would not indeed be surprising if those who allege that imitation in religious matters of the ancient Maulvis is binding, consider Mahomed *bin* Abdul Waháb as their leader. But why should those persons who keep themselves aloof from the imitation of Maulvis of still more ancient date, take him for their model?

Sixthly. Some mischievous and turbulent spirits try now and then to impress upon the minds of the British officials that the Mahomedans known by the name 'Wahábis' think it a duty of their religion to wage *jihád* against the English and kill their women and children. This notion of theirs is altogether wrong and useless, arguments in refutation of that notion having been already put forward. It is quite plain that *jihád* is not lawful without the existence of an *Imám*, and the various causes necessitating a recourse to it. To fight and kill for love of war and mischief, conquest and sovereignty, is no *jihíd* Those who intend having recourse to violent means for getting rid of the English officials or actually commit shocking acts, are certainly unacquainted with, and negligent of, the laws of Islám and the religion of Mahomed. The truth is, that the Wahábis are a set of *Mukallids** of a particular religion,

---

* Literally imitators or followers, so called because they follow parti-

because Mahomed *bin* Abdul Wahâb, their spiritual leader, was himself a *Mukallid* of the *Hambli* church. The followers of the *Hadis* do not follow any one of the many religious tenets of the *Mukallids* and the difference between them is as vast as that between the earth and the sky.

The *Ahle-Hadis* have been flourishing for a period of 1300 years. None of them has ever raised the standard of the so-called *jihád* of the present day, in any country or been ever chosen king or ruler. Most, or rather all of them have been recluses and religious devotees, thousands of miles apart from bloodshed, murder and mutiny. They do not know how to marshal a body of men and perpetrate violence and destroy the peace of the country. Hundreds and thousands of historical works are extant to this day in *Islám* dealing with the chronological accounts of the followers of the *Hadis*. In none of those works is there any mention of violence or sedition concerning them. Such is not the case with Mahomed *bin* Abdul Wahâb a detailed account of whose rebellion may be found in the history of Egypt and other books compiled by Christians and printed at Beyrout and other places. From the facts mentioned in those works I have selected some that I shall relate in this treatise, in order that people may refrain from fighting, quarrelling, and evil-doing.

What now remains to be considered is, whether the term Wahábi indicates those persons in particular who obey the *Korán* and the *Hadis* and deny imitation of the many set religious forms. Granting this to be the case it would be necessary then that the meaning attached to the term 'Wahábi' should have some signification with reference to these men. But among the *Sunni* residents in India there is

---

cular *Imáms* and their teachings, unlike the *Gair Mukallid* or *Ahl-e-Hadis* who follow the *Korán* and the *Hadis* without the mediation of any *Imám* or a spiritual guide.

not one who, obedient to the dictates of the *Korán* and the *Hadis*, has in any way in any town, opposed the British Government, prepared to carry on *jihád* himself, incited others to do the same, or been the first party in laying complaint against any *Mukallid* in any Court of justice. On the other hand those who nickname the *Sunnis* as Wahábis, are themselves the authors of such a mischief. How strange is it that these mischievous souls should be spared the nickname and considered loyal subjects of the British Crown, and in the place of these those that are abstinent, God-fearing, evil-destroying and peace-loving men, should be hauled up as Wahábis! One man causes mischief and another is accused of it.

It is in the remembrance of every one that before this, in the year 1292 A. H., I wrote a book called *Hidáyatussáil*, in page 119 of which it is written that it is impossible to give an account of the Wahábis; that their and their opponents' stories are really wonderful; and that they are wholly involved in ignorance and folly from which they cannot emerge as long as they live. In page 121 of the same book it is mentioned that it is not right to follow Mahomed *bin* Abdul Waháb or any doctor of religion whatever. In page 115 it is related that Mahomed *bin* Abdul Waháb belonged to the *Hambli* church and that we are not *Mukallids* of any religion. Our alleged dependance upon him in religious matters is, therefore, meaningless and a thing to be wondered at.

Seventhly. Mahomedan and Christian historians have both written a full account of the revolution of Nedjed that took place in the year 1212. In that year no one went to Nedjed from this country. Nay, the Indians did not know of it at all. And how could they have known it as telegraphs, railways and newspapers the result of the good Government of the British at the present day, did not exist in those days. Even at the present day, in spite of the establishment of a general system of newspapers and telegraphs, Nedjed does not send any periodical to India by which we can learn the manners and customs of the learned and the common people of that country. In fine, there is no connection, either temporal or spiritual, between the Musalman *Mowahhids** of India and the inhabitants of Nedjed. The former believe in one God, teach people good moral principles, and denounce and prevent them from, objectionable practices and customs, such as, grave-worship, beating of kettle-drums on festive occasions, nautches, taking of interest on loans and adultery. The thing is that some of the bigoted Musalmans of the *Hanafia* creed, who are extremely tenacious of their own views and given to worshipping graves, have laid, before the *Hákims*, this unfounded and evidently false accusation that the worshippers of one God are Wahábis and religious warriors, with a view to add to their own dignity, rank and respectability.

---

* Those who believe in one God; Unitarians.

CHAPTER IV.

Salim* *bin* A'mir says that a treaty existed between Máwia and the Christians of Turkey. When the period of the treaty was about to draw to its close Máwia† purposed to pillage and plunder their country. An Arab or a Turk coming to the place on horseback, exclaimed " *Alláh-o Akbar! Alláh-o Akbar!* (God is great, God is great). The treaty should be respected and the terms of the contract fulfilled." The horseman proved to be no other person than Umar *bin* Esau, a great friend of our Prophet's. Máwia asked him why he had come. He said that he had heard the Prophet of God (peace be on him and his posterity) say, " When truce exists between party and party it is proper that it should not be broken or disturbed until the period of its expiration, or the opposite party should be informed should there be an intention to commence hostilities." The narrator goes on to state that Máwia after hearing this withdrew and left the country of the Turkish Christians uninjured.

The above-mentioned facts are related in *Tirmizi* and *Abá Daúd,* works of great authority in Islám. It is plain that the above-mentioned *Hadis* does not allow violation of the terms come to between Moslem and non-Moslem nations. It was for this reason that when Abú Ráfá a messenger sent to Mahomed by the infidels of Koresh, wanted to accept *Islám* and refused to go back to his men, the Prophet said that he could not break the contract. It is related in Abú Dáúd that Mahomed caused Abú Ráfá to return to his men and said " Go now and fulfil your agreement. If you again have the desire to embrace Islám, you may come back and do so."

Such is the purport of the Prophet's words. He plainly gives it as his opinion that the violation of a contract is

---

* A *Mohaddis.*
† He was a *Sahabi, i. e.,* a companion of the Prophet.

one of the four habits which make a man a hypocrite; and that he who breaks his word is not counted a believer in one true God. He further says that he who first protects and then takes away the life of another, shall have, on the day of the general resurrection, a flag of infidelity over his head; *i. e.*, on the last day his faithlessness and insincerity will be bruited about and he himself doomed to general ignominy and shame.

Abú Horaira* relates that he heard the Prophet saying "he who does not fulfil his promises has nothing to do with me, nor have I anything to do with him." He thus excludes from *Islám* a violator of promises.

The son of Umar relates that the Prophet said "On the day of the resurrection a banner shall be fixed into the ground for those that have broken their solemn promises. They shall be called out by their names and their fathers' names, and it shall be proclaimed that the banner is the emblem of their infidelity."

Anas narrates that the Prophet said "Every promise-breaker will be known by his flag on the day of judgment."

Abi Said relates that he heard the Prophet saying "On the last day the flag of the promise-breaker shall be stuck up to his back, and be the cause of much disgrace and shame."

In *Muslim*, a work of great authority in *Islám*, it is related that Mahomed said "Every violator of promises shall have his flag longer or shorter in proportion to the amount of promises he has broken."

In fine, to fulfil one's promises and carry out the contract, be they new or old, with integrity, is the guiding principle of *Islám*. It is for this reason that when kings and rulers of the Islámic faith, possessed of wealth and power, enter into a treaty of peace with any Government,

---

* A *sahabi, i. e.*, a companion of the Prophet.

they heartily respect and observe the terms of it to their dying moment; and consider the violation of it a great sin opposed to the spirit of *Islám* and the faith.

When any Mahomedan ruler concludes a compact with any Government, his ryots are understood to be included in the same, and bound to think themselves responsible for carrying out the terms, although nothing may have been said of them at the time of the agreement. Because when the prince of a State contracts with a *Hákim* for the time being, he does so on behalf of all his subjects and dependants, not for his own private self. In a word the agreement may be looked upon as one entered into by the subjects.

It is a fact known full well to every one that during the Sepoy Mutiny when the whole native army rebelled against the British Government and began to commit as much mischief and cruelty as it could, the native Chiefs that respected their covenant did not prove faithless but remained firm in their allegiance to the reigning power. But those who acted against their plighted faith besides making themselves notorious in the eyes of the British officials, proved themselves quite alien to the principles and practices of *Islám* and the faith.

One who is insincere and violates his promises, is, according to his own religion, looked upon as having committed a great sin; and to what punishment is such a man to be ultimately doomed, will be perfectly known on the Day of Judgment. In short such a man is a loser in this as well as in the world to come.

When the laws of Mahomed enjoin the fulfilment of our promises during the whole term of a treaty, it is encumbent upon every native Prince or Chief to observe the same till the period of its close, and faithfully carry it out without a thought of violating it.

It is well known that the agreements and treaties with their several articles and propositions detailed in each, entered into by the Native Princes with the British Government, are binding upon the former in the order of descent and generation after generation. All native rulers should not, therefore, depart even a hair's breadth from their treaties, in order that they may be free from the stigma of faithlessness and insincerity in this world, and that of shame and disgrace in the next.

It is evident that only persons unacquainted with, and negligent of their religion and the beauties of *Islám*—apostates from the laws of Mahomed and *Mukallids* of a particular creed—are capable of such a faithless deed. That particular creed includes narratives on subjects both good and bad; but those persons who follow that creed, lose the very substance of their faith in their blind zeal for *taklid*.* On the other hand one acquainted with the *Korán* and the *Hadis* and with a thorough knowledge of his faith, knows full well how great is the torment and punishment prescribed in our religion for infidelity and violation of a contract, how severe the disaster and affliction in this and the next world, and how rigorous the retribution in the eyes of both God and His Prophet! The truth is, that this knowledge of his derived from the perusal of trustworthy books, besides greatly preventing and removing him from such evils, causes him to detest them.

The source of the stream of deceit and imposture and the mine of all the cheats and traitors, are to be found in *Opinion* disseminated through the Musalman world after the time of the Prophet. And the great net of all these evils is the conversation of the *Mukallids* and the interpreters of law and religion, entangled as they are in the snare of *taklíd* and inebriated by the zeal of their heretical doctrines. Such is not the case with those Mahomedans who follow the *Korán* and the *Hadis* alone. It is highly improper and forbidden in their religion to invent new ideas, mould afresh

---

* Imitation.

doctrines from the original and lay the origin of fraud and deception.

If we calmly reflect and look deeply into the state of things, it will appear that the principal source of mischief and evil prevalent in the world, is to be sought in those persons who are *Mukallids* of set religious forms in *Islám*. Those who do not worship graves and do not erect *panjás** banners, flags and other gew-gaws (in honour of the *Moharram*) but obey and follow the *Ḳoran* and the *Hadis*, are not *Waḥábis*. It would be cruelty to call them so.

No one has heard even to the present day that a *Mowahhid* obedient to the ordinances of Mahomed, the *Koran* and the *Hadis*, has ever violated his promise, been faithless or intent upon violence and rebellion. All those who proved troublesome to, and rebellious against, the British officials were *Mukallids* of the *Hanafia* church and not the followers of the *Hadis*. It was only out of sheer fraud and force that the charge of sedition was laid at the door of the latter and the rebellious termed *Waḥábis*. How were the *Hakims* imposed upon!

In the troublous times of the Mutiny when the army shook off the allegiance to the English throne, it so happened in some places that the people who were at heart enemies of the British Government but skilful enough to conceal their hatred, were regarded as loyal subjects of the Crown and rewarded with rank and dignity. It also happened that many persons starving in seclusion remote from the turbulence of men, and unable, from want of language and intercourse with the *Hakims*, from artlessness and simplicity, to advance reasons to exonerate them from the false and malicious accusations, were dragged to affliction and calamity. Some of them were hanged and some en-

---

* A model made of silver or gold representing the five fingers of Imám Hasan and Imám Hossain paraded in the streets during the *Moharram*.

tirely ruined by plunder. The stipends of some were stopped and the pensions of many withheld. The trade and transactions of some were disordered; and some were transported for life to the Andamans.

There appears to have been no wilful neglect on the part of Government in these proceedings. There are persons in every state artful enough to impose upon big officials though possessed of great quickness of apprehension. A *Hákim*, be he a Moslem or a non-Moslem is a man, and not a being possessing supernatural powers for detecting guilt. Injustice is that which is deliberately done and not that which is unknowingly committed, after great attempts have been made to discover what is right.

Laying these discussions out of the question, the doctors of *Islám*, I say, agree in asserting that violating one's promise and failing to carry it out, is a great sin. Sheikh Ibn Hajar of Mecca assigns this sin a place among the fifty-three capital sins. His discussion on the subject begins with the following *Ayat** in the sacred *Korán*—God says "fulfil your promise, it will be enquired into on the Day of Judgment." At the end of his argument he says that sheltering an infidel and then killing him, is as great a sin as the violation of an agreement. It appears from this that the violation of a treaty even with the infidels at war with us, is an enormous sin, not to speak of those that are not. At this point I can so far say with confidence that even if India be a *dárul-harb*, it would be highly sinful to violate the agreements, come to between the English Government and the native Princes. Sheikh Ibn Hajar writes in the same book that the stipulations of peace entered into between the

---

* A sentence of the *Koran*.

Musalmans and the infidels, come within the provisions of the aforesaid treaty, as has been said by several commentators (of the religious books of Musalmans).

In *Bokhari* and *Muslim* it is related that the Prophet said, "There are three kinds of persons whose enemy I am on the Day of Judgment. First, those who make an agreement and then break it. Secondly, those that sell free men and appropriate the price to themselves. Thirdly, those who get labourers to work for them and then do not give their full wages."

Muslim and others relate that on the last day when the Almighty will cause all the ancients and the moderns to be gathered together (for final judgment) he that has broken his word shall have a flag to distinguish him from others. He shall be called out thus:—"This man is the son of so and so."

Tabráni relates in his book called *Ausat*, on the authority of Anas, that the latter heard the prophet saying in his Friday oration thus:—"One who is not true to his trust, has no faith in him; and one who does not faithfully discharge his obligations, has no religion in him."

Hákim writes and vouches for the truth on the authority of *Muslim* that Mahomed said "Whichever nation violates its promises, bloodshed spreads into it"; and also that "Whoever tyrannizes over any man that has taken asylum with a Mahomedan king, appropriates a portion of his rights, oppresses him beyond what he can endure, or takes away something without his will, should consider me an enemy on the Day of Judgment."

Ibn Habbán in his work called *Sahih* declares that the prophet said, "I am displeased with those persons who, after giving shelter to certain individuals, no matter should they be infidels, take away their lives."

It is plain from the above that it is highly wrong to take away the lives of even non-Moslems, Christians for instance, that have entered into an engagement and agreement of peace with us; and that the Prophet shall be much displeased at such an act.

Abú Daúd, Nasái and Ibn Habbán say, "Whoever unjustly takes away the life of one who has taken shelter with him, shall not be able to feel the odour of Paradise, which will reach a distance travelled over in one hundred years." Another traditional account is "he who kills a man with whom he is at peace, shall not perceive the delicious fragrance of heaven which is scattered over a space requiring five hundred years to travel over."

It is mentioned in *Tirmizi* and Ibn Majja that the Prophet of God said, "He that takes the life of one who is at peace with him and therefore under the protection of God and His prophet, is himself deprived of that protection and shall not perceive the odour of Paradise although it reaches a distance requiring seventy years' duration to travel over."

It is plain from the *Hadis* above-mentioned that the violation of an agreement and putting to death a man that is on terms of peace with, and is vouchsafed protection from us, is a great sin in this world, highly displeasing to God and the prophet, and a cause of shame and disgrace before the people on the Judgment Day.

By violating an agreement a man does not only violate his own word, but that of God and His Prophet and throws great confusion in divine protection, consequently making him criminal and liable to punishment in this and the next world. May God defend us from these evils! It is stated in *Zawájir* that murder, oppression and violation of a contract in respect of those that are on terms of peace with us, have been classed in the category of capital sins and corroborated as such by the above quoted *Hadis*. This has also been testified to by learned men who put mutiny and breach of contract among them.

Hazrat Ali says "Breach of a contract implies sedition"; that is to say, violation of an agreement affecting such persons who are at peace with us, comes within the meaning of mutiny. This breach is thus narrated by the Sheikhul Islám. It is mentioned in the *Hadis* that the Prophet called this by the name of *Kabíra*, that is, a great sin. But this statement has been contradicted by Jalál Bilkaini who says that the prior *Hadises* do not corroborate the fact that the Prophet considered violation of a promise a great sin. But this much is true, that we have been severely warned against it.

It is clear from the terms 'prior *Hadises*' that he (Jalál Bilkaini) meant those of Ahmad and Bokhari already mentioned above. The following words occur in the aforesaid *Hadis* 'I am their enemy.' It is plain then that the enmity of the prophet is a great argument for the violation of a promise being a great sin.

Other *Hadises* confirm what has been mentioned above. There are a great many things which the commentators have much spoken against, and which the author of *Zawájir* has included among the great sins. In short, there is no doubt about its being a great sin. All the statements with reference to the question of breach of promise and contract have been correctly put down this day the 1st of *Rabi-ul-Auwal*, 1296 A. H.

CHAPTER V.

Rauzul Khusaib. In this book will be found some account of the rebellion of 1857 A. D., with a brief history of my own self from its beginning to the end. No sooner did I enter Cawnpore on the 5*th Rabi-ul-Auwal*, 1273 A. H. than the British Cavalry and Infantry broke into rebellion.

The disorder and the affray that followed was unrivalled. Cawnpore became a rendezvous for all the intriguing and mischievous characters of the land, who plundered the poor and oppressed the weak. It was a very undesirable state of affairs and wrought much evil (for India). I hastened to leave Cawnpore and with difficulty reached my native place Kanauj, where I rested myself and intended to devote my time in worshipping our Creator in retirement and peace. But I was mistaken. Providence had intended otherwise. The people of the town had offered no opposition nor had they rebelled in the least against the British power. The Sepoys of the Nawab of Farrakhabad, a town towards the north-western corner of Kanauj, made a small fight with the British troops. The blame rested with their ill-bred chief, and as a punishment the whole town was plundered. The Sikhs and the Panjabis plundered our houses too and left nothing with us to be cared for.

Next day news spread all over the town that a general massacre would follow. The disciples of my respected father took me with all other men and women to Bilgram, five kós distant from Kanauj. In Bilgram we took our lodgings in Mahalla Mardánpurá. I had one black-coloured suit to conceal my body, had dry bread once a day to satisfy the cravings of the stomach and the well-water of a mosque to quench my thirst.

During this period I learnt by-heart a few chapters from the Korán. After this I went to Mirzapur. It was here that I received a *parwáná** from Nawab Sikandar Begam, inviting me to Bhopál. I took my journey to Bhopál *viâ* Jabbalpore. When I reached Bhopál towards the end of the month of *Safar*, I received another order to leave Bhopál at once. After a week's stay I took my departure from the town and in my way reached Tonk. There I be-

---

* A letter from a man of authority to his dependant.

came the guest of Syed Hamiduddin, now deceased. The Waziruddaulá Bahadur insisted upon my accepting a vacancy with a small remuneration. After eight months' stay in Tonk I was favoured with another letter from Nawab Sikandar Begam apologising for what had happened on the previous occasion of my visit. I reached Bhopál on the 13th Moharram 1275 A. H. and was very kindly received by the Begam who paid all the expenses of my journey to Bhopál and asked me to forget the past. I was entrusted with the duty of writing a history of Bhopál and making bye-laws for conducting the general business of the State. Shortly after, the management of the Sulaimani Madrasa was entrusted to me. I thought this arrangement very fortunate for me, as it afforded me every opportunity of pursuing my literary course and employing my time in my favourite studies. This state of affairs lasted one year when Abdul Ali, *Mir* Munshi* of the State was dismissed, and I was put in his place against my will. I received the title of Khán and *Mír Dabir*.†

I was not pleased with this post, but I had to acquiesce in the arrangement. One cannot avoid his fate, decrees of Providence are ever executed by force.

Next year the present ruler of Bhopál honoured me by giving me her hand in marriage. The Government of India was first informed of the proposed match and its permission obtained. This connection proved to me a source of honours. I received the title of *Motamadul Mahám*‡ and with it a *jágir*§ yielding Rs. 24,000 per annum, a grand *khilat*‖ valued at Rs. 10,000, with horses, elephants, palan-

---

* Chief Secretary.

† The same as *Mír Munshi*.

‡ The second minister of Bhopál is so called. *Chargé d' affaires*.

§ An assignment by a Chief of an estate or of the land revenue on certain villages.

‖ A robe of honour.

quins and swords. Shortly afterwards the British Government conferred upon me the title 'Nawáb Amír-ul-Mulk Wálájáh' and fixed for me a salute of 17 guns.

Over and above all this I got an assignment of land yielding one lakh a year. In short I lost my former independence and became a bondman.

The magnanimity, generosity and kindliness of heart of the present ruler of Bhopál, being well known, many evil-minded persons tried to take advantage of this fact to carry on their intrigues.

Three or four years ago, some men out of sheer ingratitude, animosity and envy, tried to disgrace me in the eyes of the authorities, by charging me with Wahábiism. They averred that the *Khutbá**** enjoining *jihád*, had proceeded from me. But the authorities and the representatives of Her Majesty the Empress of India, convinced of the good intentions and loyalty of this State in general and of the writer individually, their calumny proved of no avail, and it was known that their charges were baseless and groundless. Otherwise they would have taken the blood of an innocent person upon their heads. A reader of the books and histories of the past well knows that such imputations and false-hoods often spring out from personal motives and animosities. But as the adage is 'One who sinks a well for another, falls into it himself,' so such people often fall victims to their own fraud. Still they do not take a warning. Leaving *Kharjis*, *Rafziz*, thieves and dishonest men, they gird up their loins to attack the followers of the *Hadis* and give them the appellations of *Wahabis*, *Bághis*† *Ghazis*‡ and *Tághís*.§

---

* A sermon or oration delivered after Divine service every Friday, in which the preacher blesses Mahomod, his successors, and the reigning Mahomedan sovereign.

† Rebels.

‡ A hero, particularly so if he has fought against and slain one or more infidels.

§ Rebels.

Whereas it is quite clear that one who goes by the path pointed out by the prophet and does not follow particular tenets, has nothing to do with Wahabiism, or imitating another form of Mahomedanism.

Liberty of belief is a blessing which among the Mahomedans the *Sunnis* alone possess. To bind oneself to any particular form of tenets, such as those held by the *Necharis*,* the *Mukallids*, the *Bidatis*, the *Hanofis*, and so forth, is a calamity and an occasion for entertaining inimical feelings towards the British Government.

What we are sorry for, is that the mischief-mongers and traitors of our age, impose upon Government and accuse of disaffection the poor and peaceful Mahomedans who pass their days in prayers, fastings, pilgrimages and the giving of *zakat*,† who shun bad habits and do not lay themselves open to charges of ingratitude and desertion. Anything untrue or unfair does not enter their minds. They are the well-wishers in words and deeds of the authorities and the public. They think it their greatest duty as taught by their religion, to keep to their promises, never to break their words, to obey the authorities and to swear fidelity to their chief.

Now it requires very little proof to show that these virtues are possessed by the *Ahl-e-Sunnat* and are scarcely found among the *Bidatis*. The young and the old all know that the British Government has no concern with anybody's beard, *chughá*‡ or turban. To keep one's trousers above the ankle or the collar running down to the middle of the

---

* This word is loosely applied to signify atheists. It is derived from the English word, 'nature' and hence it should literally mean followers of the laws of Nature.

† Alms, a portion of a Musalman's property given in charity agreeably to the rules laid down in the *Korán*.

‡ A kind of long gown.

chest, to avoid nautch parties and the company of public women and pimps, can do no sort of harm to the Government. What then, I am tempted to ask, have these matters to do with Wahabiism and rebellion against the British throne? When the *Ahl-e-Sunnat* detest the very name of Wahabiism, do not confine themselves to the tenets of any particular school, to call them Wahábis or identify them as followers of a set form of Mahomedanism, is to tease and oppress them. As for ourselves we enjoy freedom of thought and follow only the *Korán* and the sayings of the Prophet.

If by the term Wahabi be meant one that is an enemy of the British Government, and one that thinks it his duty to wage *jehád* against the Government, I should briefly say that no Mahomedan can deny that the question of *jehád* is treated in his religious books, or that he believes in the propriety of the precept in connection with it. But he must acknowledge that the making of *jehád* must be preceded by the existence of certain conditions that make it lawful. These conditions are set forth in the books of *Fekah** and *Sunnat*, and *jehád* is not allowed if these do not exist; and a man who undertakes *jehád* under circumstances when the necessary conditions do not exist acts against the behests of his own religion.

In short there cannot be a greater mistake than to think that the mere existence of precepts respecting *jehád* in the religious works of the Mahomedans or a knowledge and acquaintance of the students with this doctrine, is rebellious against the British Government. If the mentioning of religious books of the Mahomedans as a duty, were to be considered as an offence against the State, it would affect all Mahomedans of whatever denomination or belief. There appears to be no reason why the *Sunnis* alone should be marked out and stigmatized as Wahabis. And if the treat-

---

* Theology; knowledge of law and religion.

ment of the question in the religious books, is no offence, as it is really not, all the Mohamedans are equally innocent of such a charge.

The same can be said of other questions similar to the one alluded to above. Can any body say that the question is not treated in (1) *Dur-e-Mukhtár* (2) *Fatawai Almgiri* (3) *Ḳazi Khan* (4) *Kanz* (5) *Hidaya* (6) *Kudúri* (7) *Shámi* and (8) *Hamawi;* and that it is only to be found in the religious books of *Sunnis* called by their enemies Wahabis? Whereas among the books said to have especial connection with the Wahabis and which have also been enumerated by Dr. Hunter as such, as for instance, *Takwiat-ul-Imán, Nasuhat-ul-Muslimin, Ketábut-tamhid, Iḳteza-e-Serát-e-Mustaḳim* &c. &c., not even a mention is made of the question of *jehád*. Having regard to equity and common sense, if the question of *jehád* is not touched in those books, how can the readers of such books, whose practice conforms to the doctrines laid down in them, be termed Wahabis? These books denounce the evils of worshipping many gods but one: dangerous innovations are prohibited, cleanliness recommended and honest and fair dealings inculcated. At the same time it is a well observed fact that Mahomedans of different denominations and belief call one another Wahabis. Everybody with a tittle of common sense can understand that these things have nothing to do with entertaining inimical feelings against the British Government.

Those who give the name 'Wahabis' to the Indian Musulmans and connect them with Mahomed *bin* Abdul Wahab of Nedjed, forget that both the Mahomedan and Christian historians are at one in saying that this teacher of Nedjed never came to India, nor did the people of India ever stand in the relation of disciples to him. Full particulars regarding the point can be found in *Asír-ul-Adhár*, history of Syria and many compilations of Christian writers; and I have dwelt upon the subject in *Taj-e-Mukallal*.

These writings will clearly show that he invited only the people inhabiting the neighbourhood of Hejaz to accept his tenets and his doctrines spread only in that quarter. He made *jehád* upon the wandering tribes of the Mahomedans of that part of the country and had nothing to do with other sects.

In short if good bearing, propriety of conduct and avoidance from intrigue and mischief, be called Wahabiism, it would be strangling justice and common sense to hold such an opinion. If by Wahabiism be meant seeking a quarrel with the British Government then those, be they Hindus or Mahomedans, who have opposed the British from the commencement of their rule, and were given to plunder and bloodshed during the Mutiny and on different other occasions, should be termed Wahabis; and there appears to be no reason why persons who are pious and virtuous should be marked out as such. As regards this matter the real facts, we believe, are that it is merely a political trick played by a certain class of lawless, disaffected souls who want to save themselves and bring others to trouble by accusing them of Wahabiism. They want to screen their enmity and rebellion by this means. Thinking over this subject, we cannot forbear exclaiming that it is no doubt true that many things that have made a noise all round, are wholly groundless. It cannot but be accepted that there can be no better friends and well-wishers of the British Government than people who are honest and well-behaved, inasmuch as their rule of conduct is based upon justice and honesty, and that it is rivetted upon their attention that rebellion is unlawful and breach of promise unsacred. The tenets of their faith have for their basis the public good, general security and protection of interests. In religious matters they enjoy and exercise the same liberty of conscience which has been so often the subject of proclamations under the British rule, more particularly on the occasion of the assumption of the title of Empress by Her Majesty the Queen, at Delhi when the grandest Darbar was held.

The many treatises and pamphlets that have been compiled hitherto, in refutation of the doctrines held by the adherents of the *Taklíd* system, make it clear that their opponents are free from following any set form of tenets ascribed to particular Mahomedan divines and commentators. On the contrary all the books written by the *Mukallids* in defence, give forth in unmistakeable terms that the writers and their party are the followers of the set form of tenets; that they think it their duty to follow the footsteps of recognized teachers; that they have nothing to do with freedom of belief; and that they commend it only to the British Government or such under its rule who declare that they enjoy and exercise freedom in matters appertaining to their religion. Now it would be a proper question to ask ' Who are likely to be the enemies of the British rule, whether those that are the followers of the set forms in religion, or those whose views are liberal and free ? Great is the difference between the two, and only those who do not try to think over the subject and understand it, make foolish mistakes.

CHAPTER VI.

Translation of Taj Mokallal. This book contains a record of the Islamic religion and the memoirs of wealthy personages in ancient times. It is a historical work in the Arabic language. It seems desirable to give here some accounts of the personages referred to in that book.

Ibn Saúd. His name was Mahomed and he lived in Nedjed. According to the *'Asárul Adhár* he was descended from the Sheikhs of Arabia called Anza, the name of a tribe. He was the head of the Masalikh tribe and was connected with the tribes Wáel, Taglab, and Shamrán. He was good-natured, munificent and wise. His grandfather Saúd was the head of his family and lived at Dara'iya among his own clan. He was one of the officers of *Ibn* Ummár, the ruler of Ayána.

When Mahomed *bin* Abdul Wahab declared his Wahabi faith, Karámta rebelled and took refuge with *Ibn* Saúd who accepted the religion of the former and prepared for his aid. Mahomed *bin* Abdul Waháb promised that his ally should be the ruler of the towns of Nedjed. This took place in the year 1760 A. D. *Ibn* Saúd then took to wife the daughter of Mahomed *bin* Abdul Wahab; and many of his clansmen followed him in accepting the religion of the latter. Thus Wahabiism spread through his countries and many of his people began to profess it. His power increased day by day and many gathered round him as their chief. A battle took place between him and *Ibn* Daás, in which the latter was defeated, who fled to Katif where he died. At this time the power and dominion of *Ibn* Saúd extended over all the towns and villages of Nedjed towards the south. Encouraged by the successes of all his undertakings, he decided to make himself ruler of all the territories of Nedjed. He now invaded and conquered 'Arár Karmati. Then again mustering a great force he led it against Ḳasím, Ahsáe and 'Asír, which all yielded to his mighty power. He now died and left his son Saúd in the possession of a large kingdom.

Ibn Saúd managed and governed his kingdom well and did many works of public utility. Thus the promise of Mahomed *bin* Abdul Wahab that he should be the ruler of all the towns of Nedjed, was fulfilled. The inhabitants of the adjacent territories began to fear him and be afraid of opposing and fighting him. He was magnanimous, brave, sensible, acute and courteous, a man of great literary culture and a good orator. He populated Dara'iya and built mosques and other edifices. The people loved him and delighted in his society, by reason of his cheerful disposition and charming conversation. He could not endure oppression, extortion and bloodshed over his ryots. He treated them tenderly and mildly. But he went on propagating Wahabiism, calling himself an *Amír** and putting the reins of authority in matters concerning the faith, into the hands of *Ibn* Abdul Wahab. He died in the year 1790 A. D.

The work that contains the above-mentioned accounts was written by a learned Christian theologian and published at Beyrout. It relates about Mahomed *bin* Saúd, his religious Chief Mahomed *bin* Abdul Wahab and the years in which they flourished.

Abduil Aziz son of Mahomed *bin* Saúd comes next. It is mentioned in the *Ásárul Adhar* that he was appointed *Khalífa* or Caliph by Mahomed his father. He guided himself by the laws and religion of his father, and followed his footsteps in the government of the kingdom. He made great endeavours to propagate Wahabiism and was always engaged in difficult tasks and severe battles. He was very powerful and brave. He was a great theologian in his religion. From the Persian Gulf down to Hejaz the people yielded to his power and authority. After strengthening

---

* Lord or Master.

and confirming himself in his own country, he prepared to reduce all the Arab clans to his subjection and conquer the provinces of Hejaz. Gálib, *Sharif*** of Mecca, opposed him, which led to a war between them. This war began in the year 1792 or 1794 and continued for a long time. After a few months the Wahabis overthrew Mecca and Medina.

Abdul Aziz had now thoughts of Ḳatíf. He took it and put the inhabitants to the sword. He now coveted the Bahrain Islands. He conquered them as well as all the adjacent islands. The maritime towns of the Persian Gulf and those lying on the gulf of Oman, offered their submission and acquiesced in his authority.

He now despatched his army to Oman whose ruler Saíd after sustaining a defeat, fled to Muscat and shut himself in the fort. The army, however, pursued him to the very gates of Muscat and laid a prolonged siege to the fort. Tired of his beleaguered state, Saíd sued for peace. A treaty was at last concluded between the belligerents by which Saíd agreed to pay the *Jezzia*† every year. It was also stipulated that the privileges of the Wahabis over the mosques at Muscat should be recognized.

At this time the Wahabis were looting the regions of Basra and plundering the Arab tribes in districts lying round about it. This state of things continued till the year 1797 A. D.

In the same year Sulaiman Pásha of Bagdád sent a large army, raised from the inhabitants of Zafar, Baní Shamar and Muntafaj, against Abdul Aziz. The army turned towards Dara'iya and in the way directed its attention upon Ahsáe. It invested this fort for a period of one month, whose commandant apprised Abdul Aziz of the ap-

---

* A title given to the ruler or governor of Mecca.
† A tribute, capitation tax levied by the Musalmáns on their subjects of another faith.

proaching danger. The latter immediately came out of Nedjed with a formidable force to repel the invader. But a treaty of peace for a term of six years was concluded between the parties. Sulaiman Pasha returned to Bagdád after the treaty was ratified.

Abdul Aziz mustering an army despatched it to the *Mashhad** of Imám Hosain and himself accompanied the van. He passed by the banks of the Euphrates. The inhabitants of Ḳawít being afraid of him, submitted to his arms and offered many slaves and presents. For this reason he refraimed from killing and extirpating them.

He now sent a part of his army to Zobair, Súḳ, Shawíh and Samáwá, in order to reduce those towns also; and himself reached the *Mashhad* of Ali (may God be pleased with him) which he surrounded. The ruler of the place remained shut up in the fort for a long time. After the conquest of this fortress, Abdul Azíz turned his attention to *Karbala*† where he spread carnage and plunder. The furnitures found in the shrine were pronounced by him *mobáh*‡ for his soldiers. The city was for the most part depopulated.

After the termination of this conflict and on his return to Dara'iya, Abdul Aziz was attacked by a large Turkish army sent against him by the Governor of Bagdad. He met the army at a short distance from his city and after severe fighting and bloodshed put the soldiers to the rout.

In the same year he fought with Gálib the *Sharíf* of Mecca. The next year he again collected a force and sent it against Táef, a city in Hejáz, where he was victorious after spilling much blood. He subjected to a general massacre

---

* A place of the martyrdom of.

† The name of a place in 'Iráḳ, where Hosain the son of 'Alí suffered martyrdom, and where his tomb is still visited by pilgrims.

‡ Any indifferent action, which incurs neither praise nor blame; allowable.

the people of Karbalá and plundered their wealth and properties.

In the same year he took Kanfaza, situated at a seven days' journey south of Jeddah. In the year 1804, Abdul Aziz formed an army of Wahabis and giving his son Saúd the command of the advanced guard, despatched it to Mecca. On its arrival the army invested the Mecca fort for three months and caused great consternation among the besieged. When their provisions began to fail the Meccans surrendered. Gálib, the *Sharif* of Mecca, being thus defeated went away to Jeddah.

Abdul Aziz entered Mecca in the month of *Naisán** and paid all the respect and reverence due to the sanctity of the place. Some say that he massacred the Chiefs and gentry of Mecca and uncovered the *Kábá;* and that he forced the people to become converts to Wahabiism.

He now proceeded with his army to Jeddah which gave in after a siege of eleven days. Gálib, the *Sharif*, was compelled to pay his submission, which he did and offered much riches and presents to the conqueror.

Abdul Aziz was murdered during the same interval. The story told about his death is that in the middle of the same year, he was one day engaged in his prayers. Abdul Kádir, a Persian belonging to the *Shia* sect, attacked him and gave him so severe a cut of the sword between his shoulders that he fell to the ground and began to wallow in his blood. His men ran after the assassin and pierced his body with their spears.

With reference to the cause of the murder, historians relate that the king of Persia caused Abdul Aziz to be assassinated as the latter had seized the towns of Katif and the Bahrein islands formerly belonging to Persia, and had

---

* The name of the seventh Syrian month corresponding to *Baisakh* of the Hindus and April of the English.

laid waste the *Mashhad* of Imam Hosain. As the Persian king had no power to cope with him in open battle, he devised the plan of thus having him secretly despatched by the hands of Abdul Ḳádir. This man came at first to Dara'iya where he pretended great virtuousness and chastity, and used to pray at the mosques in order the more successfully to conceal and carry out his bloody resolve.

Abdul Aziz was also very punctual in his prayers, and said each of the five daily prayers at its appointed time. This regularity and punctuality in prayers were the rule with other Wahabi theologians.

Some say that Abdul Kadir murdered Abdul Aziz in revenge for the death of his sons whom the latter had killed with his own sword at Karbala.

The third in order is Saúd son of Abdul Azíz who ascended his father's throne in the year 1804. The *'Asárul Adhár* thus gives an account of his reign and character :— He was wise and generous, brave and liberal. He was a learned man and versed in literature. He was hardy and courageous enough to undertake many arduous tasks. Of all his brothers he was the most loved by his father for his valour and bravery. His father sent him on many occasions to countries far and near at the head of armies, and success in many cases crowned his arms. He was just, mild and religious and was for this reason much loved by his subjects high and low. He was noted for his despatch of business, but used to sentence criminals to severe punishments. He defended the Fast of *Ramzan* and tried much to effect the abolition of the practice of divorce.

Sa'd was ever the constant and faithful servant of Saúd during the days of his wealth and authority. When Sá'd died, his family was reduced to great misfortune, so much so, that separation took place between the members.

Saúd was a man possessed of great wealth and a large army. He wore a thick beard and moustaches. Hence the citizens used to call him *Abî-ul-Shawárib* or the Father of moustaches. He had eight sons from the first wife and three from the second.

When Abdul Aziz, Saúd's father, breathed his last, Sa'd was at Hejaz engaged in war with Gálib, the *Sharíf* of Mecca. He cut off the communications of the opposite army, defeated Gálib and obliged him to submit to his authority. Gálib returned to Mecca and finding the Wahabis unguarded, resolved to surprise them. But Saúd received him with great respect and reverence and kept him near his own person.

Again, hostilities commenced between Saúd and Baní Sarb. After committing much havoc and bloodshed in the country of his antagonist, Saúd came to Yambó whose citizens yielded to his authority.

He now marched upon Medina where he fixed the *Jezzia* upon the inhabitants. He uncovered the holy sepulchre of the Prophet, plundered the buried treasures of the tomb and took them all away to Dara'iya. It is said that the treasures obtained were carried away upon sixty camels.

The shrine of Abi Bakr and that of Umar met with the same fate. He appointed Namar-*bin*-Sheikh-bani-Harb governor of Medina and forced the people to accept Wahabiism. Saúd now purposed to knock down the dome of the Prophet's tomb, but happily did not put this resolve into execution. He ordered that no one should go on pilgrimage to Mecca except the Wahábís; and prohibited the Turks from visiting the place. For some years none could go as a pilgrim to Mecca, the Syrians and the Persians included. Most of the pilgrims were thus debarred from visiting the holy shrine.

At the end of the year 1804 Saúd sent Abú Nuḳtá, the chief of the Assyrians, with his infantry to the towns of Saná-e Yaman. He spilt much blood of the inhabitants of those towns. After devastating Lohaya and Hodeida, he returned to his own country. Hamúd the master of Saná-e became a convert to Wahabiism in order that his town might be safe from the danger. All the towns of Hejaz consented to do homage to Saúd, whose power now spread throughout Arabia except Hadramaut and a few villages of Yaman. In short his dominion extended both in length and breadth.

Saúd sent his army to the town of Basra at different times. At one time his army reaching that town committed great bloodshed in the country lying between the Euphrates and the Tigris.

He sent Harak his slave towards the Syrian desert, who, after sanguinary engagements, pursued the flying enemy up to Aleppo. A part of his army crossed the Euphrates, and spread plunder, rapine and bloodshed throughout the land. When it was only a short way from Bagdad a war broke out between Abu Nukta, the Assyrian and Hamúd, the governor of Sanáe.

In the year 1809, Yusuf Pasha became the master of Syria. He tried his utmost to break the power of the Wahábís, but without avail. In the same year a British naval squadron entered the Persian Gulf and began to shell the tents, which were all destroyed. The men who lived in those tents were pirates who robbed Englishmen and plundered their vessels.

In the year 1810 A. D. Saúd with six thousand Horse invaded Syria, where he made a great havoc of the lives of the inhabitants. He devastated forty-five Syrian towns on his way to Damascus which now remained at a two days' journey. The inhabitants were seized with alarm and Yusuf, the Governor, had not the power to oppose such a formidable foe. But Saúd did not push his victory forward and withdrew.

He now received an information that some of the *Sardárs** of the towns of Háik refused compliance with his

---

* Chiefs or headmen.

authority. He immediately despatched an army which began to plunder and lay waste the country and after forcing its way into the town of Hatwa, put the young and the old to the sword. Of the ten thousand inhabitants no one survived this indiscriminate slaughter.

When Wahabiism and the dread of the pomp and power of Saúd began to be on the ascent, Sultan Mahmúd Khan of Turkey resolved to crush him and thus save the people from the recurrence of his wicked deeds. He wrote to Mahomed Ali Pasha, the Khedive of Egypt, to expel him from Hejáz and annihilate his authority and dominion over the sacred temples of Mecca and Medina. The Khedive consequently began to gather men and provisions, and, when a very large army was formed, sent it to Arabia under the command of his son Tirsún Pasha. The fleet consisting of twenty ships of war passed by the Suez and reached the Yambó seaport. The army landed in the month of *Tashrin*. In the beginning of the year 1811 A. D., it left Yambó for Medina. In the way Badar and Safrae were taken by storm. Abdullah the son of Saúd and his brother met the army at New Mazík nearly twenty miles distant from Medina. A bloody battle ensued in which the army of the Khedive was defeated. The Wahábis took all the stores, tents and baggages and captured four guns with all the munitions of war.

Tirsún Pasha again came to Nedjed and reached Medina in the beginning of *Tashrin Auwal* in the year 1812 and surrounded it. In the Second *Tashrin* of the same year, he entered it and ordered his men to ransack the town and massacre the Wahábis. Some of the latter shut themselves up in the fort; and it was only when the provisions were all consumed that they asked quarter for their lives. Tirsún spared them. But no sooner had they been out of the fort and gone far away from Medina, than the army attacked them and killed all of them except such as fled away.

In the year 1814 A. D. Tirsún conquered Mecca and

Jeddah, and a severe battle took place between him and the Wahábis. In the same year the Egyptians took possession of Kanfaza.

After a short time the Wahábis attacked the town and the Egyptians were obliged to fly for their lives. On entering it the Wahábis went round the usual course of murder and bloodshed. At the same time Saúd *bin* Abdul Aziz whose accounts I have been narrating, died of fever. This happened on 8th *Jamadi-ul-Auwal** 1229, corresponding with the 28th of *Naisán* in the year 1814 A. D. He was sixty-eight years of age at the time of his death.

The fourth is the account of Abdullah son of the same Saúd whose history has been narrated above. He was brave and enjoyed his father's confidence in many matters of State. He was more magnanimous, more courageous but more aggressive and less resolute, than his father. In the battle which took place between him and Mahomed Ali Pasha, the Khedive of Egypt, he was utterly routed. The Khedive now came to Hejáz to enquire about the state of his army, and with its help subjugated the Wahábis and shed much blood in the towns. He then freed the people from their hands.

He now returned to Mecca. In the year 1818 he required Abdullah to sign a treaty with the condition that the things taken as booty from the Shrine of the prophet be returned; otherwise the army of the Khedive should descend upon Daráiya and destroy it altogether. Abdullah refused to comply with the term and marched towards Nedjed to meet Tirsún Pasha. The latter was encamped at Khabra in the outskirts of Ḳasím and he himself encamped at Shannan, a few hours' march from Khabra; cut off the communications of the Egyptians and blockaded them on all sides. The Egyptians dismayed by his overwhelming

---

* The fifth month of the lunar year of the Mahomedans.

force, sued for peace. In this they played false upon Abdullah who consented to come to terms. The treaty between them embraced the following conditions: That the Wahábis should not be opposed. That they should be permitted to perform the pilgrimage without let or hindrance. That the Egyptians should leave Kasím and return those Arab chiefs who, violating their compact with Abdullah, had combined with them. And that they should recognize the allegiance to the Sultan. Besides these, there were many other conditions.

Tirsún Pasha left Khabra and withdrew towards Rás with his army. From there he went to Medina which he entered in the month of *Kharbarán* in the year 1815. He did not find his father there as he had left for Egypt on some urgent business.

Abdullah sent two messengers to the Khedive of Egypt to have a legal warrant confirming the treaty. But the latter refused to comply with his request, and said that as long as Ahsée, a charming and fruitful country of the Wahábís, was not made over to the Empire, he could not ratify the treaty. Consequently the ambassadors returned unsuccessful.

This treachery of the Egyptians exasperated Abdullah who now prepared to fight them with a large army. This state of things continued till 1816 A. D.

In the month of *Áb* in the same year, Ibráhím Pasha son of Mahomed Ali Pasha, came to Hejáz with a formidable army. He fought some very hard battles with Abdullah in order to regain the lost towns. God gave him the victory and defeat to the Wahábis. The battle of Máwia was among the number and occurred on 12th of *Yár* 1817. The other battles were those of Aníza and Shakra which took place on the 14th *Kanún Sáni*, 1818. After these, a battle was fought at Zirmá and another at Daráiya. Abdullah collected men and a good store of provisions and ensconced himself in the fort with all his army. Ibráhím Pasha kept him invested for a long time. The fort at last opened its gates and Ibráhím Pasha entered it, taking Abdullah and his family prisoners. None escaped except a son of his by a Turkish woman.

Some say that when Abdullah despaired of his deliverance and found Daráiya all destroyed by the shower of cannon balls, he asked for quarter which was granted. This took place on the 8th of *Zikád* 1244 A. H., corresponding with *Balól* in the year 1818 A. D. In fine, Abdullah came to Ibráhím and threw himself on his mercy entreating protection and one day's respite. Ibráhím received him with great respect and gave him the required time. The next day in accordance with the terms agreed upon, Abdullah was sent to Egypt under the escort and surveillance of the army. He started on 14th *Zikád* and reached Mahomed Ali Pasha, Khedive of Egypt, on the 18th Moharram. The Khedive treated him with much attention and ceremony and bestowing on him a robe of honour, sent him on to the Sublime Porte. He arrived there on the 17th of *Safar*, 16th of *Kánún Auwal,* in the year 1818. He was pinioned and then put to death. Kharandara and Abdul Azíz *bin* Sulmán who wrote an account of this proceeding were thrown into prison.

CHAPTER VII.

At page 226, Chapter IV, of a work called *Mirat-al-Wazia fil Kurratularzia*, written by Colonel Yousecandek (?), an American, in which he speaks about the Arabian towns, is thus narrated the history of Mahomed *bin* Abdul Waháb :—

"The Wahábí band became strong in the beginning of this decade. It derived its origin from a Tamímí man, or in other words, Mahomed *bin* Abdul Waháb himself. He was among the descendants of Ali and belonged to the Masalikh clan. A part of this clan inhabits the environs of Zobaid on the Persian Gulf. Mahomed *bin* Abdul Waháb lived at Daráiya in Nedjed. Saúd *bin* Abdul Azíz was the Governor of Nedjed in those days. He was the *Sheikh* or chief of the town and belonged to the clan called *Rabi'atul-jars*. So that Saúd combined with *Ibn* Abdul Waháb and in the year 1760 A. D. began to propagate his teachings. He was succeeded by his son Abdul Aziz who repulsed two large armies sent against him by the vizier of Bagdád. In the year 1794 A. D., he overthrew another army led under the standard of Zaid, son of Masaid, *Sharíf* of Mecca. This Wahábí band conquered Irák and after attacking the mosque of Ali, reduced it to ruins. In the year 1804 A. D. Abdul Aziz sent his son Saúd with a force of 12,000 men, to Táif and Mecca, over which the commander succeeded in making himself a master. He now marched with his army to Jeddah where, during the siege, he heard that his father Abdul Azíz was dead. He consequently came back to Dara'iya. In the same year he went to Hejaz and took possession of Medina and conquered all the countries in its vicinity. He ruled over them till the year 1815 A. D., when Ibrahim Pasha, the Governor of Egypt, prepared to drive him out. He overthrew Saúd in many battles and at last drove him from Hejaz. Saúd died of fever at Dara'iya when he was fifty years of age. His descendants ruled and still rule over Nedjed. Their chief town is Riadh. They are all Wahábís."

This book was compiled in the year 1852 and revised in 1871 A. D. The author of it also writes that Nedjed is the name of a country that lies near Syria on the north, Irak on the east, Hejaz on the west and Yamama on the south. It is a very delightful spot in Arabia—a spot upon which the Arabian poets have pronounced the highest encomiums.

An elevated ground in Nedjed, which was the park or pleasure-ground of Kalíb *bin* Wáel *bin* Rabia, proved ultimately the scene of his death which took place in a battle fought here and known by the name 'battle of Basus.' This battle is proverbially famous in Arabia.

The Akáz mountain is situated in Nedjed. Nowhere else has the Arabic tongue been preserved in its purity and fluency as there.

In fine, no one appears to have written in any book or history anything more than what I have mentioned in these seven chapters with regard to them. The facts enumerated correspond with the statement and investigation of Christian theologians, decidedly admitting of no further investigation.

It appears from the above-mentioned facts that there is no Indian Musalman that is a follower of Wahábiism; because the doings of the Wahábis in Arabia generally and Mecca and Medina particularly, and the molestations received at their hands by the people of Hejaz and the inhabitants of those holy cities, have never been perpetrated by the Musalmans of India. None in India can be so audacious.

It also appears that the Wahábi sedition was completely crushed in 1818 A. D.; and no one rich or poor in Nedjed, did afterwards rise in rebellion. On the other hand in the same year, the misrule consequent on the dissensions and a spirit of defiance among the Native Chiefs, were all set to rights by the good Government of the British. On the one side riot and murder were rife at the hands of Nawab Amir Khan, the Chief of Tonk; on the other, Holkar, the Raja of Indore, had raised tumult and uproar in Khándésh and other countries. The plunder and loot at the hands of the Pindarees* grew more and more frequent. Wazir Mahomed Khan Bahadur† kept all the materials and instruments of war ready at Malwa.

Thus in every part of India were Native Chiefs oppressing the ryots and trying to extend their own territories. But the English Government made treaties with them suitable to their rank and dignity; quietly seated them on their respective *gaddis*; and gave them written agreements granting them territories to be permanently governed and enjoyed by them generation after generation. These treaties exist to the present day and both parties have been acting in accordance with the terms.

The treaty with the Bhopal State was concluded in the year 1818 A. D., *i. e.*, when the Wahábi disturbance in Nedjed was brought to its close. No one since that date has offered any opposition to, or rebelled against, the British Government. On the other hand during the Indian Mutiny when most of the British subjects proved disloyal, the Native Chiefs, true to the terms of their treaties, rendered as much assistance to Government in provisions, men and money, as lay in their power. The Nawab Sikandar Bégam of Bhopal sent her army as far as Jhansi and gave assistance in grain and other things from her State. In the same manner did

---

* Name of the hordes of freebooters who infested Central India previous to the English supremacy.

† Prime minister of Bhopal during the reigns of Nawab Hiyat Muhammad Khan and Nawab Ghaus Muhammad Khan, but virtually the absolute ruler of Bhopal for twenty years in the reigns of both the Nawabs. He was held in great estimation by the English. He died in the year 1816 A. D.

the Nawáb Sháh Jahán Bégam, during the Cábul campaign, offer her assistance in men and money to the British Government; as also in the current year on the breaking out of the Egyptian war, did Her Highness sympathise in every way with Government and express her desire to offer assistance. When Arabi Pasha was vanquished and Egypt restored to undisputed authority of Towfík, Her Highness the Bégam ordered salutes to be fired from the Fataḥgaṛh* fort, as an indication of her pleasure at the event, and wrote a letter congratulating the Viceroy on the same.

On other occasions also has Her Highness in union with myself, first of all shown her good-will and expressed her sincere desire to assist the Government. This expression of devotion has always been appreciated by the British Government and elicited letters and telegrams conveying the thanks of the Viceroy, at different times.

Description of a recent Phenomenon.

Since the date 15th September 1882, after the conquest of Egypt, a comet appears in the East at 4 o'clock A. M. Its tail resembling an elevated lance, is very long and broad. The head, called the nucleus, is small like a minute star and near the eastern horizon. The broad tail is inclined towards the South and is evenly white. The comet which appeared after the Indian Mutiny, was of a quite different shape. It was not so large. Its tail was rendered visible owing to the constellation of a few small stars that gave it a cometary appearance. The tail of this comet is one white column of light and does not appear to be due to the assemblage of other stars.

We of *Islám* do not, like astrologers, believe in the influence of stars. We rather regard them as so many ornaments of the heavens, the instruments for the punishment

---

* The fort of Bhopal, built by Dóst Mahomed Khan, founder of the Bhopal family, about A. D. 1721

of evil spirits and the signs to guide oneself by, on land and sea. But, according to our books, the frequency of such a phenomenon as the comet, indicates the appearance of Imám Mehdi* and the descent of the Messiah on this earth at a not very distant date.

The thirteenth century of ours has now only ten months to expire. The fourteenth century will begin from 1301 A. H. and 1884 of the Christian era. The descent of Jesus Christ, the appearance of Imám Mehdi and the liberation of Dajjal†, will take place in the first part of the century. And because these incidents shall happen at a time when the world will have been filled with oppression, and when art and government will have reached their perfection, it appears that the day of the descent is not far off.

The force of religious fanaticism is felt everywhere. The *Nécharis* have raised a cry of their own. These people declare themselves Musalmans only for show. There are also Pandits among the Hindus who, having been founders of new religions, wish all men to be their followers.

An intermediate religion has sprung up at Lakhnow. The world has now been full enough of such evils. For a period of six or seven years bloodshed is sure to happen in some place or other. Some rebel against their old masters. Some unreasonably accuse others as rebellious Wahábis. Some deny Wahábiism altogether. Some wish for universal peace. Some follow a particular religion. Some are intent upon oppressing the poor Mahomedans. Some support atheism. Some expound religious questions by the principles of philosophy. Some, being themselves *Mukallids* of set forms of faith, zealously try to overthrow the *Sunnis*. Some characterize the followers of the *Hadís* as *Rafzís*. Some consider the *Mukallids* as lost and benighted. Some seize upon the

---

* The name of the twelfth and last Imam who is said to be still living, but invisible, and will appear at the approach of the Day of Judgment.

† Antichrist. Literally, a liar, an impostor.

properties and means of livelihood of others by forgery. Some seek access to the Chiefs and the *Hákims* by deceptions and false representations. Some try to harm their own benefactors. In some places father and son are at war with each other. Son-in-law and mother-in-law are at difference. The daughter quarrels with her mother. Men having no right, try to establish it while the rightful are silent.

In short it is simply impossible to enumerate all these evils prevailing by hundreds and thousands in all towns and countries, not to speak of Arabia and Persia. If the day of the general resurrection does not come even now, when will it come at all? It is hard to pass one's life in these days when dangers from within and without are so innumerable.

CHAPTER VIII.

Acting under the instigation of the servants of the late Nawáb Ḳudsia Bégam and in obedience to the request of Syed Hasan, Syed Ahmad, Munshi Latifullah Khan and Syed Abdulláh of Surat, the *Times of India* in its issue dated the 28th February 1880, published the folllowing correspondence :—

"Sir,—We the undersigned lovers of peace request your goodness to insert the following article in your valuable paper and oblige.

"We are sorry and astonished to learn from the Arabic newspaper *Aljuwáeb*, dated Constantinople, 25th Moharram, 1297 A, H., or 8th January 1880, that S'iddiḳ Hasan Khán Sáhib, a Wahábi gentleman, husband of H. H. the Begam of Bhopal, G. C. S. I., has forwarded two or three books of his own composition to be published and sold by that Press. The titles of the books indicate that they are against the popular and peaceful creed of the orthodox Moslems continued on for the last twelve centuries up to this day, and the books are in favour of Wahábiism tending to mischief and rebellious excitement in the Moslem world. We are astonished because the principal seat of Islam, *i. e.*, Constantinople, allows this sort of mischief to take its root in the capital, whereas Sultán Mahmood Khan II and Sultán Abdul Aziz Khán, as well as the late Mahomed Ali, Pasha of Egypt, punished and drove Wahábiism from their jurisdiction."

"Syed Ahmad Ul Edroos
Latifulla Khan, *Munshi*.
Syed Abdulla, *Son of the Hon'ble Syed.*
Hasan Edroos, C. S. I.

Surat, Feb. 18*th*."

The editor of the *Aljuwaeb* then retorted immediately afterwards and silenced the *Times of India* and pointed out its mistake.

The *Times of India* was, however, again prevailed upon by Syed Hasan and others to give out that I was a Wahábi. This was seriously taken notice of by the Bhópál State and communicated to the Political Agent at Sehore and the Agent to the Governor-General for Central India, at Indore. The paper at last gave up publishing such a false and malicious report.

There is no mention of rebellion or *jihád* in those books. In fact they have nothing to do with religion whatever. They deal with the science of history, philology, and derivation and signification of words.

In the month of *Zikád* 1298 A. H. Syed Hasan died.

In connection with the fact above related, it is necessary to know what in the world Wahábiism is, which has been made the cause of so much fuss and bustle, and which every man, entertaining feelings of animosity against another, has tried to use as an instrument to injure and defame him before the *Hákims*.

According to the investigations of Christian theologians contained in such works as the *Asárul-Ádhár*, &c. &c., published at Beyrout, it appears that Máhomed *bin* Saúd was the name of an *Amír* of Nedjed. A man named Mahomed Abdul Waháb flourished in his time. In the year 1760 A. D. this man happened to be at variance with the Bohra tribe on a certain question of religion. He was assisted by Mahomed *bin* Saúd who died after 1790 A. D. Mahomed *bin* Saúd was succeeded by his son Abdul Aziz. He, like his father, popularized the religion of Mahomed *bin* Abdul Waháb. He opened hostilities in Arabia and the countries round about Nedjed. In the year 1792 or 1794 A. D., Mecca, Medina and other towns were taken possession of by him. His son Saúd now succeeded him in 1804 A. D. and maintained the same system of religion which his father had done. In accordance with the command of Sultán Mahmúd of Turkey, Mahomed Ali, Pasha of Egypt, attacked and defeated him in the year 1811 A. D. He died in 1814 A. D., aged 63 years. Saúd was succeeded by his son Abdullah. He fought with Ibrahim Pasha, son of Mahomed Ali, Pasha of Egypt. He was at last taken prisoner and sent to Constantinople where he died in prison. This war ended in the year 1244 A. H. or 1818 A. D.

Thus, the origin of Wahábiism appears to have been laid in Nedjed and the outlying districts; and nowhere else did that religion ever obtain a footing. It also appears from books compiled by learned Christians at Beyrout that Mahomed *bin* Abdul Waháb followed the tenets of Imam Hambal.

Since the period of Saúd and his allies' death no one has to the present day emigrated to Nedjed. The Musalmans of India have always been either *Shias* or *Hanafis*. Their manners and customs have not been derived from Nedjed—a fact no history can contradict. They have not ever been the pupils or religious disciples of the people of that country. They have no books of the Nedjedians current in India.

But I see that in some towns some people call others Wahábis and write treatises in refutation of the theories of one another. After deep meditation I have found out the cause of this to be mutual hatred.

Among the seventy-three tribes in *Islám*, all of whom have been numbered by Mahomedan doctors in their books, there is none by the name of 'Wahábí.' Those who have been bruited about as Wahábis in India by their enemies, repudiate that title altogether and no trace whatever is found of their connection with Nedjed.

The question arises what those *masalas* (precepts of Mahomed) are which have condemned one tribe as heretics and another as Wahábis. After much reflection I have found out those to be several in number. Some of them have reference to *Akáid** and others to divine worship. In those *masalas* there is nothing that relate to *jihád*.

Dr. Hunter has written a work in which he gives the number of *masalas* relating to *jihád* as seven, and the number of books bearing upon it as fourteen. But he is mistaken with respect to these *masalas*, as is also manifest from the criticism of Syed Ahmad Khan, C. S. I., which was printed in London together with its translation in English. The exact number of books mentioned is also wrong. He has named some books which do not treat of Wahábiism at all; such as *Dur-e-Mukhtar*.

Those who do not worship tombs, who do not offer presents and supplications to the dead, who do not bow down to the opinions of Maulvis and dervises, who do not celebrate the *Majlis-e-Maulúd*, and who do not make *Tázías*, are not the followers of any particular set up form of religion. They preach against theft, deception, extortion, adultery, violation of a promise and such heinous crimes. They are the followers of that religion which has come down uninterruptedly for twelve hundred years, when no one knew the name of any other faith but *Islám*. An account of this is found narrated in the *Kórán* and the *Hadises*.

These *Hadises* have at various times, during the past seventy years or more, been published in Calcutta, Delhi, Bombay, Egypt and other places. They are being published even now. The object of these books is to instil into the minds of men a desire to worship God, to keep fast, to visit the holy Mecca and perform other religious duties, at the same time refraining from vicious acts. There are hundreds of such books and treatises in Arabic and other languages, extant to the present day since hundreds of years. They are neither *fourteen* nor forty in number.

---

* Articles of faith. Plural of *akída*, faith.

A man named Fazal Rasul who lived in Budaon, first gave the name of Wahabis to the Indian Musalmans, which in course of time became general. Those that were viciously inclined impressed upon the minds of the *Hákims* that the Wahabis were the enemies of the British throne. They have, however, found out after much enquiry that merely calling a man a Wahabi, does not show that he is an enemy of the reigning power, so long as he does not commit some seditious acts. But they have come to this conclusion after a long time. There was a time when the mere calling a man a Wahabi was sure to call him to a severe account. But fortunately such is not the case now.

Syed Ahmad Shah of Nasirabad, Bareily, was a man who taught people the worship of God and the observance of the fast and prevented them from many sins and turbulent deeds. He left the North-West Provinces and fought with the Sikhs in the Panjab. He was reported a Wahabi and an enemy of Government by Fazal Rasúl of Budaon; although he had been to Calcutta where many Musalman soldiers of the English army had chosen to make him their spiritual guide. He never entertained a design of warring against Government nor did the Supreme Power interfere with him, notwithstanding that he took seven hundred men with him from Calcutta on the occasion of his pilgrimage to Mecca and wandered about preaching from place to place in India accompanied by thousands of his disciples. The writings of Syed Ahmad Khan, C. S. I. are a sufficient guarantee for the truth of this statement.

The accounts of Syed Ahmad Shah of Bareily and those of the Wahabis, the *Masalas* treating of *jihád* and *Hijrat**, the question whether India is a *dár-ul-harb* or *dár-ul-Islám*, and the accounts of those works which the people regard as the books of the Wahabis, have been well dealt with in

---

* Departure from one's country and friends; flight.

the treatise written in Urdu and English by Syed Ahmad Khan, C. S. I. and printed and published in London, in refutation of Dr. Hunter's animadversions. Syed Ahmad Khan being held in confidence and regarded a loyal subject of the British throne, his writings are therefore the more reliable. As for myself I have neither seen Syed Ahmad Shah or been his contemporary. Of course I have heard and read about him in Syed Ahmad Khan's work.

I happened, very lately, to come across the following reply of the Government of the Panjab to a petition signed by several hundreds of the Wahabis, asking for the redress of their grievances :—

"From—Lepel Griffin, Esquire, Secretary to Government, Panjab."

"To—Maulvis Muhammad Husain, Rahimulla, and three hundred other petitioners.

"I am directed to reply on the part of the Honorable the Lieutenant-Governor to the petition signed by about 300 persons, and purporting to express the opinion and wishes of several thousands belonging to that sect of the Muhammadan faith commonly known as the Wahabi.

2. "The petitioners declare that, although they are as loyal as any other of Her Majesty's subjects, they are, on the suspicion of disloyalty, exposed to many annoyances and placed under many disabilities; that they are not allowed the free exercise of their religion which the Queen's proclamation has promised to all; that they are excluded from the mosques and from Mahomedan processions, and are viewed by the people generally, following the lead of the Government, with dislike and distrust. That it is even impossible for a Wahabi to obtain justice in the law courts; for that immediately on his sect being known the Judge is prejudiced against him. In conclusion they pray that they may be restored to the confidence of the Government; that people may be prevented from holding and treating them

as disloyal; that they may be relieved from Police surveillance and permitted the free exercise of their religion, also that those Government officials professing Wahabi opinions may no longer be suspected and debarred from promotion.

3. "The Lieutenant-Governor is glad that the petitioners have come forward to state their grievances, and is quite prepared to reply without reserve to their appeal.

"In the first place, I am directed to observe that although the petitioners repudiate the name of Wahabi, yet it is the one by which they are commonly known, and, so far as it is used in this letter, is not intended as a term of reproach.

4. "The Lieutenant-Governor further is very pleased to observe that the petitioners altogether deny any idea of disloyalty to Her Majesty the Queen, and entirely disavow the acts and opinions of those Wahabis who, for many years past, have been engaged in secret intrigue or open resistance to the British Government. His Honor is quite willing to accept these assurances. The class which the petitioners represent has for some time past behaved, in the Panjab, in a most loyal and peaceable manner; and the Lieutenant-Governor assures them that so long as they continue to act like good subjects of the Queen, the Government will regard them with favour equal to that shown to any other class of Her Majesty's subjects. If the sect known as Wahabis have been regarded with suspicion, it is due to the fact that many of its members have, chiefly in other parts of India, acted in a disloyal manner, especially in rendering assistance to the rebel colony at Malka on the Hazara border. His Honor does not, however, desire to visit the offences of others upon the petitioners or upon any one who, like them, profess active loyalty and act as orderly subjects.

5. "With reference to any disabilities in the matter of religious worship, I am to observe that His Honor the Lieutenant-Governor desires in every way to carry out the

declarations of the Government securing to the professors of every creed the unfettered exercise of their worship so long as the public peace is not endangered. But any opposition to the public observance of the Wahabi form of worship is due to the body of Muhammadans themselves, and not to the Government. The Wahabis are a sect of dissenters from the form of Muhammadanism ordinarily practised in the Panjab, and while they may claim the free practice of their ceremonies and the preaching of their distinctive doctrines in their own mosques, they cannot insist upon the use of the mosques which have been built by the money and for the use of orthodox Muhammadans.

6. "So far as police regulations are concerned, the Wahabis are at present under no special surveillance, and the Lieutenant-Governor is happy to believe, from the assurances of the petitioners, that this will in the future continue unnecessary.

7. "The Government further does not look with disfavour upon its officials who belong to the sect of the petitioners, nor debar them from promotion. All it requires in its servants is zeal in the discharge of their duties and active loyalty. As a proof of this, I am to mention that Syad Hidayet Ali, Tahsildar of Batala one of the most prominent of the Wahabi party, has lately been promoted an Extra Assistant Commissioner, and at least one other of the same sect, whose services have been often approved, is on the list for similar promotion at some convenient time.

8. "The Lieutenant-Governor is glad to have had this opportunity of assuring the petitioners that so long as their conduct is as orderly and as well disposed as now, they will not be regarded by the Government with disfavour.

9. "This correspondence will be circulated for the information of the Commissioners of Divisions.

"Dated Murree, the 10th November 1876."

The *Civil and Military Gazette* in its issue, dated the 8th August 1879, supported the opinions of the Panjab Government in the following words :—

"It would be difficult to get any one to believe now-a-days in the old theory that rebellion was the chief motive of the Wahabi movement. Yet the traditional belief had some grounds for its existence. During the first period of Indian Wahabiism, 1822 to 1830, its apostle Syud Ahmed and Maulvi Ismail preached their *jihád* against the Sikhs. In 1857, many of them acted in concert with the rebels; and subsequently with the Sittana fanatics, whose misdeeds led to one of the most important of our border Campaigns. The Wahabi doctors would, however, say that the *jihád* of 1822-30 was justified by Sikh oppression, and point to Maulvi Mahbub Ali's conduct during the Mutiny as being indicative of the feeling of all intelligent Musalmans—Wahabis included—towards a perfectly tolerant and benign Government like that of British India. Summoned by Bukht Khan to sign a proclamation of *jihád*, the Maulvi not only declared that the enterprise would constitute a violation of the true principles of Islám, but he manfully protested against the barbarities perpetrated by the rebel leaders. In short, he took up the position afterwards vindicated by a present Member of the Viceregal Council, the Hon'ble Syud Ahmed Khan, C. S. I., in the little volume which he wrote by way of reply to Dr. Hunter. Our reason for adverting to these facts is to draw attention to a monthly publication issued by the 'Mowahids,' as they are called, or Wahabis of Lahore, who appear to be pretty numerous both in the city and the surrounding districts. The last number of the *Ishaat-us-Sunnat* contains an article on *jihád*, in which it is stated that disloyalty towards such a Government as that of British India would be regarded as a breach of the Wahabi religious principles. The object of the article is to show that not one of the circumstances which would justify a *jehád* exists under the present rule. Maulvi Mahomed Hussein, the conductor of the monthly periodical, is the author of a pamphlet published two or three years ago with the object of showing that Wahabiism is nothing more nor less than what the Hon'ble Syud Ahmed Khan has already described it, *viz.*, the Puritanism of Islám. Maulvi Mahomed, we believe, has travelled over India, for the purpose of getting the principal *ulmás** to join in his declaration of Wahabi professions of loyalty towards the Indian Government. Our readers may remember that two or three years ago, a loyal declaration signed by several hundreds of the Lahore Wahabis was addressed to the Lieutenant-Governor of the Panjab."

Again the *Civil and Military Gazette*, dated October 14th, 1879, wrote to the following effect—

"The September number of the *Ishaat-us-Sunnat*, a Wahabi publication, issued at Lahore, contains an article in which the murder of Sir Louis Cavaguari and his followers is described as a crime abhorrent to the religious feelings and ideas of every true Musalman. The writer enforces his arguments by texts from the Koran and other authoritative books, as also from the example of the prophet himself. Here is an instance. Au Rafia was sent as an ambassador to Mahomed by the unbelievers of Mecca. But when he heard Mahomed preach, he embraced Islám, and refused to return to Mecca. Whereupon the Prophet spoke of the sacred character of ambassadors, declined to sanction Au Rafia's breach of duty, and persuaded him to go back. On another occasion an ambassador who claimed to be a prophet, and was an enemy of the new faith, expressed his contempt for Islám, in the presence of Mahomed : but the Prophet merely replied that but for the respect with which Islám regarded all ambassadors, his presumptuous language might have cost him his life. The writer adds that this respect for the

---

* Plural of *alim*, a learned man.

representatives of other nations was enjoined upon his followers by the Prophet, in the last moments of his life."

While writing this chapter I happened to come across a vernacalar newspaper called the *Terahwin Sadi*, Vol. III, No. 5, of the year 1298 A. H., and published at Agra, whose contents ran thus :

"I chanced to sojourn at Allahabad for a few days. I met with some young men there who were engrossed with the idea—' That a book should be written on the defects of the custom and religion of the Musalmans and a catalogue of the names of those *álims* called *Mahaddises* of both ancient and modern times, be prepared with a view to criticise their writings. That those *álims* should be spoken of as Wahabis.' The title chosen for such a book is—*The Register for the refutation of Wahabis.*

"This is blackening paper and no profitable work. If the book is intended to please and flatter the Government, it is a different thing altogether involving a different mode of procedure and no pain. Many books of this description have been already published. One of them, I well remember, is that written by Maulvi Abdul Latif Khan Bahadur, Deputy Magistrate and Deputy Collector, Calcutta, in the year 1287 A. H. or 1871 A. D., when some Englishmen had begun to seriously discuss the proposition that Wahabiism might be a source of danger to the British rule in India; and which, for a long time, engaged the attention of the well-wishers of the country, until at last it was discontinued by Government interference. The Maulvi wrote that book on the part of the Musalman public with a view to silence the prevailing notions of the times. In that book he detailed *fatwás* of the Mahomedan doctors of most parts of India and also those of Mecca and Medina, with a view to show that, according to those *fatwás* opposition to Government was unlawful, and that no Mahomedan, from the present circumstances of India, could entertain a doubt with regard to its being a *dár-ul-Islám.*

"The excellent Nawáb Wálá Jáh Amír-ul-Mulk, Sayyad Muhammad Siddiḳ Hasan Khan Bahadur of Bhopal, of exalted title and erudite learning, profound in religious literature, a gifted expounder of the *Hadises* and unparalleled commentator of the *Korán*, has also approved that treatise, and ordered it to be generally distributed. He has himself very carefully and with a completeness of detail, reviewed this *masala* in several of his works, in which he unequivocally condemns rebellion against the British Government in the present state of India, as sacrilegious. He has very beautifully rejected the interpretations differently put upon the *masala* and acted up to accordingly, by the former *álims* like Shah Abdul Aziz and others. Two years before this, the Nawab had already made a mention of this *masala* in *Mawáid-ul-Awáid*, evidencing much excellence and research. And like other works this book obtained a wide circulation between India, Egypt and Constantinople, and between Peshawar and Teheran. Any gentleman desiring to have it, may have it at his command from us.

"When such a book as that above-mentioned, written by such a princely *álim* as is himself a very reliable authority in matters concerning the faith, and that written by Maulvi Abdul Latif Khan Bahadur, detailing the different *fatwás* on the subject, are already in the field, what necessity and gain have the mediocre people of indifferent qualifications, to intermeddle in the dispute, to pass unfounded strictures upon their own religious books, and thus render themselves an object of mockery in the eyes of others. As for instance. I am a *Sunni*. If any man were to call me a Wahabi (a title utterly devoid of foundation and which no one has yet adopted), with a view to stir up the suspicions of Government, cause it to use terms unsuited to my rank and dignity, or incite it to pass such adverse criticisms upon the doctrines of my faith as were likely to produce religious perturbations—such a man, if prosecuted, cannot escape ruin and destruction. What is the use then of doing things betraying folly and attended with loss. It is far better for persons possessed of too meagre an attainment to enable them to join in religious disquisitions, to desist from the discussion or first acquire sufficient learning to share in the controversy. Then and not till then should one be possessed of such ambitions."

Afterwards in No. 6, Vol. IV, of *Asháat-us-Sunnat*, I found, on perusal, the following in the beginning:—" From page 164 to the end is worth the attention of Government."

The paper alluded to above was dated *Rajab** 1298 A. H. or June 1881 A. D. I went through it. The opinion of the Editor of that paper concerning the reform in the mode of religious disputations, the concord and union among the Musalmans, and the Government of India generally, appears to me to be quite correct and appropriate. Were Government to pay attention to the suggestions contained in that paper, distrust should give place to confidence in the people, and, in lieu of the religious fanaticism which has got entire possession of the nobles and the plebeians, a good government of the country should be secured.

According to the *Hanafia* creed I have represented India as a *dár-ul-Islám* in several of my publications, and mentioned in them the absence in this country of the conditions for *jihád*, a fact alluded to in the ' *Térahwín Sadi*.'

The book containing the expression of my views was published before I had the knowledge of the discussion that had arisen in Calcutta on the subject, which Maulvi Abdul Latif Khan Bahadur took so much pains in, and which, subsequently, led to the publication of a criticism by Syed Ahmad Khan Bahadur, C. S. I., on Dr. Hunter's book.

There has never been any religious discussion in any

---

* The seventh month of the Mahomedan year : it is also called *Rajáb-ul-morajjab*, or the sacred *Rajab*, because in the time of paganism it was unlawful to go to war in that month.

of the sects at Bhopal; and consequently the officials of this State have had no knowledge of the religious disputes prevailing in other towns and no desire to look into such books.

On the other hand in the year 1298 A. H., owing to a political necessity, I read the criticisms and the newspaper alluded to above, because I found the statements therein contained just in keeping with the principles of Moslems in general and those of the *Ahl-e-Hadis* in particular.

Here I must thank Khaja Muhammad Yusuf Ali Sahib, Manager, '*Térahwín Sadi*,' for his having, without my knowledge, favourably reviewed my previous and present works.

It is pleasant to think that on the basis of the same arguments as have been used by those who have shown that India is a *dár-ul-harb*, it can also be proved that *jihád* is never justifiable in this country. It is a mere fight of words. In like manner in my work *Ibrat* which discusses the *masalas* of *jihád* and *hijrat*, and which was written at the time of the Russo-Turkish war, gives the same conditions for the waging of a holy war, as are *non est* at the present day.

In another book called the *Aklail*, I have copied the following Arabic sentence of my tutor's tutor, Kazi Muhammad *bin* Ali Shaukáni (may the mercy of God be upon him). "The least degree of justice for an *Imám* is to try, like the British Government, to conduce to the general quiet, and be a well-wisher and peace-maker of the generality of mankind."

In short the occurrence of the *masalas* of *jihád* in ancient and modern books of *Islám* and the mention of the authoritativeness of *jihád* against the enemies of the faithful, can never lead to war and rebellion against the British Power.

It is the case in every faith and persuasion that when a learned man sits to investigate, ascertain, compose or compile a book respecting his own creed, he necessarily puts down in it what has been proved by reason and argument in that creed. As for instance, in the *Korán*, the *Hadises* and the *Fikah-e-Islám*, we have the *Kitab-ul-Jihád* with all the *masalas* virtues and commands which are usually learned and taught. From this work no fear of the occurrence of a rebellion can be entertained, as long as the author, having provided himself with the outward signs of rebellion, does not claim the *Imámat*, seek *jihád* and spread a general spirit of revolt in the country.

At the time of the Mutiny there were hundreds of rebels who, according to the histories of the country, are said and heard to have been the bitterest enemies of the former and the present *Hákims*. They were perfectly illiterate and their leaders and chiefs also did not know what is *jihád* and its excellence—not to speak of the mutinous army. The object of their rebellion was not to carry on the *jihád* of *Islám*. Had it been so, no *álim* in *Islám* could have at all supported or encouraged them in that treasonable crime.

Be it whatever it might, the charge of Wahabiism and that of carrying on of a religious war, against the *álims* of the *Hadises*, be they ancients or moderns, is altogether an erroneous fancy; and no wise, experienced and discerning man can for a moment believe that the learned will justify *jihád* against the British Government, in the present state of India, or think that the conditions for it exist; except those *mullás* who have had no perfect knowledge of their religion and no correct information,

As for myself I had no necessity whatever to raise my pen in this discussion. But a book entitled the '*Maeza Hasna*' (good admonitions), a compendium of Friday *khutbás*,* was published at Bhópál. This book contains the *khut-*

---

* Sermons or orations delivered after Divine service every Friday, in which the preacher blesses Mahomed, his successors, and the reigning Mahomedan sovereign.

bás read on Fridays all the year round, five *khutbás* a month, by the former *álims*, extending over hundreds of years; as those of *Ibn* Jauzi and Mahomed *bin* Ahmad of Yaman and others. In the last part of it, the work contains a *khutba* on the *gazv**, the compilation of Maulvi Mahomed Ismail, along with the *khutbás* relating to the *Kasúf* (eclipse of the sun), *Khasúf* (eclipse of the moon), *Istiska* (draught), *nikáh* (marriage), &c., &c., just in accordance with the system observed in different countries in the compilation of *khutbás*. For this my enemies called me a Wahabi. However, an answer to this accusation has already been given in *Girbál*, the history of Bhopal.

I have seen neither Maulvi Mahomed Ismail nor his time, nor have I found any mention of *jihád* in any of his works. Even this *khutbá* does not contain any order for waging *jihád* with the English Government. It enumerates the virtues of *jihád* like other books in *Islám*. Such *khutbas* and books abound in the histories of Mahomedan kings; and the collections of *khutbas* are found published in various countries.

Eight years before the publication of the *Maeza Hasna*, I had declared in my work called *Hidáyatus-Sáel* to the effect that I was not bound to follow either Mahomed *bin* Abdul Wahab of Nedjed or Mahomed Ismail of Delhi. Even if any Musalman were to take any *masala* relating to *shirk*†, *bidat* and *taklid*, from the work of any Mahomedan doctor and make it an article of his creed, and the writer of it his spiritual guide, he could not harm any Government or kingdom until he did not stand charged with violence and rebellion.

Alims of all castes and creeds borrow thoughts, derive advantages, and deduce arguments from the writings of one

---

* War against the infidels.
† Ascribing plurality to the Deity.

another. This is no crime either by religion or by law. But when this was advanced against me as an accusation, and reported by way of a malicious information, of course, I got as much offended and enraged as any man would at a false report and an unfounded charge. I was therefore obliged to narrate the history of Wahabiism in this chapter.

To call me a Wahabi is the same thing as abusing me; and to connect me with those individuals termed Wahabis, for religious or private hatred, by some persons—individuals who never were Wahabis, who never rebelled against the English Government, and who never gave *fatwás* of *jihád* in India is purely an act of great injustice.

In concurrence with the views expressed by Syed Ahmad Khan in his reply to Dr. Hunter, and his criticisms on the same, I say that Syed Ahmad Shah of Bareily who was reported a Wahabi by Fazal Rasúl of Budaon, did not unite in his person the attributes of a learned Maulvi. He was a dervise of the Sayyad tribe. He was a disciple and followed the teachings of Shah Abdul Aziz of Delhi, the latter practising the religion of his father Shah Waliullah, *Mohaddis*, of Delhi.

Shah Abdul Aziz used to preach and impart good lessons to the people. His exhortations brought thousands of the illiterate Indians into the right way. He and his father flourished either before or very near the time of the Nedjedian disturbance. But none have dared to call them Wahabis. They had no knowledge of the religion of the Nedjedians. They did not make any mention of Wahabiism in any of their works. They were rather unacquainted with the name and the religion.

Similarly Syed Ahmad Shah of Bareily and his disciples do not say anything of the Wahabis in any of their writings. Even the *masalas* of *jihád* do not find a place in them. A book written by Syed Ahmad Shah, named *Sirát-e-Mustakím* (a right road), formerly published in Calcutta and twice again at the present time at Delhi and Meerut, contains rules as to how a dervise should lead his life. Another work called *Takwiat-ul-Imán* (strength of faith), compiled by Maulvi Ismail of Delhi, condemns *shirk* and *bidat*. Throughout the work no trace is to be found of the Wahabis or the *masalas* of *jihád*.

Similarly, the *Rah-e-Sunnat* and *Hidayat-ul-Mominín*. (A guide for Moslems) deal with the vices of heresy and *Tazia* worship.

Tazia worship is heretical even in the *Shia* faith. Were Government to collect and go through all the books, it is believed, it would not be able to find in any one of these a *masala* treating of *jihád* or rebellion against the British Throne, or anything calculated to engender misrule.

Syed Ahmad Khan Bahadur, C. S. I., is mistaken in calling Syed Ahmad Shah, his pupils and disciples, by the term Wahabis and in mentioning that the Wahabis are found in all sects, the *Hanafia* and other creeds; but that they do not consider *jihád* with the British Government legal. In the concluding part of the sentence he says that he can point out the names of many Government servants than whom there are no better well-wishers or faithful friends—who, notwithstanding, openly and unhesitatingly call themselves Wahabis and in a way pride themselves in the appellation. Syed Ahmad Khan Bahadur evidently alludes to himself in the above-mentioned sentence, because he considers himself a Wahabi at heart.

In my opinion the Mahomedans of the world may be divided into two classes. The *Ahl-e-Sunnat* and *Jamaat*, also called *Ahl-e-Hadis*, and the *Mukallids* of particular forms of faith. The latter are divided into *Hanafis*, *Sháfais*, *Málikis*, and *Hamblis*. The man that was born in Nedjed and agreeably to whose doctrines Mahomed *bin* Saúd of Nedjed, fought with the Bóhras, the Bedouins and the Musalmans of Arabia, belonged to the *Hambli* creed. This has been verified by the histories of both Moslems and Christians. How then can the *Ahl-e-Hadis* be Wahabis?

Moreover, the term has quite a new import in every town of India. With the followers and disciples of Fazal Rasul of Budaon, a Wahabi indicates one who does not worship tombs and spiritual teachers and objects to paganistic practices. In Lakhnow, Cawnpore and Delhi, a Wahabi is one who does not follow the *Hanafia* church and does not bind himself by the doctrines of a particular religious teaching; but obeys the *Kórán* and *Hadis* alone. In Bombay and other towns the term signifies one who does not believe in Sheikh Abdul Ḳádir Gíláni, and who, when aboard a steamer, does not shout out 'Edroos' and invoke his assistance in times of trouble and anxiety. In Hydrabad and the Deccan the term designates an individual who does not take the fermented juice of date-trees, and does not attend fairs and the anniversaries of the dead. In some places a Wahabi is considered to be one who wears a long beard and cuts off his moustachios, and puts on high *paijamas* (trousers). While in others, one who does not observe *Mahfil-e-Miláď** and the *Gyárahwin*† of Sheikh Abdul Kadir, is dubbed a Wahabi. In Bhopál the term indicates one who does not make *tazias*, who does not visit Ajmere Makunpúr, who does not take the food offered to the dead as *Nazar* and *Niyáz*‡, but who reads and makes others read, the translation of the sacred *Ḳorán*.

Thus in every town the signification of the term 'Wahabi' varies. In the eyes of the British Government and according to the researches of Dr. Hunter, 'Wahabiism' is a synonym for rebellion, and 'Wahabi' but another name for

---

* A religious meeting to commemorate the birth of the Prophet.

† A festival celebrated on the 11th of Rabiul Auwal in commemoration of the birth of Sheikh Abdul Ḳádir Giláni.

‡ Gifts or presents of sweetmeats made to the souls of holy men at their shrines or religious festivals.

a rebel. Syed Ahmud Khan Bahadur has very well refuted this erroneous meaning of the term, and his criticisms have been justly and wisely accepted by Government.

I have to say in this place that the *masala* of *jihád* is a thing which is believed in by all the Moslems of the world of whatever caste or creed, and which, by a wonderful coincidence, occurs unmodified in all the books of *Islám*, without the least discrepancy. There are few *masalas* in *Islám* that have not given rise to diverse opinions or statements, except the one on *jihád* continued unchanged on to the present day. When this *masalá* is recognized by all Mahomedans, it is unreasonable to attach the name ' Wahabis ' to them, and then think it to mean rebellion and *jihád*. If it were reasonable to do so, then all the Mahomedan world in general and not the few Indian Musalmans in particular would be Wahabis.

Dur-e Mukhtár, *Hidáyá*, *Sharah Wakáyá*, *Fatáwá-e-Alamgiri*, *Háshia Shámi*, &c. &c., are all books of the *Hanafia* church. The *masala* of *jihad* is to be found treated in all of them.

The *Hanafis* deny being Wahabis and probably the Government does not call them so. Neither do the Nedjedians consider them their co-religionists; although those books have been published at various times and acted up to by all the *Hanafis*.

Similarly the *masala* of *jihád* occurs in six or seven other books of the Hadis; such as, *Mautá*, *Bokhári*, *Muslim*, *Abú Dáúd*, *Tirmizi*, *Nasái*, and *Ibn Májá*. This *masala* also occurs in the religious books of the *Shias*, with this difference that they have deferred the *jihád* to the appearance of Imám Mehdi; whereas the *Sunnis* have put it off until the conditions for it do not exist. These conditions are not such as can exist at all times. Their existence is as difficult as the appearance of Imam Mehdi.

Let us leave aside these books. The sacred *Korán*

which is the root of all the sects of *Islám*, has the virtues of *jihád* narrated in it. The rendering of that sacred book into the Urdu, the Persian, the Turki, the Pashto, the German, the French, the Roman, the Greek, the Sanskrit, the Latin, and the English, languages, exists all over the world. The custom of reading that sacred book is so generally prevalent among the Musalmans, that every man and woman whether young or old, goes through a portion of it once every day by way of a religious duty. But up to this day never has any one by perusing it launched into *jihád* or rebellion. The reason is that the conditions do not exist.

Let us now leave aside the present period and look back to that five hundred years ago. When Tamerlane invaded and took many Moslem and non-Moslem countries, the doctors of *Islám*, instead of designating the battles that he had fought by the name of *jihád*, characterized them all as mischievous wars. So that when wars waged by Musalman kings five hundred years before, could not, for absence of the conditions, be termed *jihád*, how can the anarchy and rebellion got up everywhere in these days by illiterate persons, be so styled? How can these wars, the conditions for waging which have been enumerated in all the books of *Islám*, be worthy of those rewards promised in the holy *Korán*, the *Hadís* and the *Fikah*?

In the same way the wars carried on by Mahomed *bin* Saúd, king of Nedjid, and his descendants, were not *jihád*. And the people of Mecca, Medina and Yaman, the headquarters of *Islám*, were displeased with him. Those who rebelled against the British Government and violated their plighted faith during the Mutiny, were not actuated by motives of *jihád* but of insurrection. Hindus, Musalmans, Mahrattas, Rajputs, and men of all creeds had taken part in the rising. No Mahomedan friendly or inimical to them, can call them Wahabis.

As Syed Ahmad Khan Bahadur has discussed the question of *jihád* in his reply to Dr. Hunter, so I had, before the knowledge of this fact, denied Wahabiism altogether, *first*, in my work called *Hidayatus-sáel;* and *secondly*, in another entitled *Rauz-e-Khásaib.* Thirdly, in my work known as *Mawaid-ul-Awaid*, I had mentioned that to violate one's promise was an egregious sin and that *jihád* was not lawful in Hindustan. *Fourthly*, I had written in my work entitled *Táj-e-Mokollal,* an account of the Wahabis from the histories of Christian divines. The gist of them all is that the rising of the people during the Indian Mutiny, is termed *jihád* only by those who are unacquainted with the origin of the Islamic faith, and who wish to cause disorder in the country and destroy the prevailing peace.

As long as an *Imám* of the Koresh family and no other, possessing all the attributes enjoined in the *Shará*, is not selected with the unanimous consent of the wise and the principal men of a country—an *Imam* whom they think it their bounden duty to obey—and all the conditions for levying *Jezzias,* and pressing people to become Musalmans do not exist, so long *jihád* is impossible. Such an *Imám* has not been found in the world for hundreds of years and the conditions of *jihád* have always been wanting. The mere existence of the *masala* of *jihád* with the non-existence of its conditions, in the books of *Islám* does not make any Musalman a *jihádi*, a Wahabi, or a rebel.

Moreover, a spirit of rebellion is not peculiar to the Mahomedans alone. In every tribe anarchists and rebels are to be found. They are the enemies of the Wahabis. It is a notorious fact that the Wahabis of Nedjed consider it right to kill all the Mahomedans of the world and plunder their properties. So in their eyes we are worthy of being massacred. How then is Wahabiism saddled upon us?

In Afghanistan and countries near it, the people are rigid *Hanafis* and the inveterate foes of those few Musalmans whom mischievous persons have designated as Wahabis. They have been at war with the Government for four years. Have they therefore become Wahabis? No Mahomedan of India or any other country has, up to the present day, considered them in that light. Men who, like Syed Ahmad Shah of Bareily and his followers, have been forcibly so termed, did not even utter the name of *jihád* against the British Government on the frontiers of Hindustan, a fact which has been well sifted in the criticism on Dr. Hunter's book.

When the whole of Arabia resounded with the noise of the Nedjedian disturbance, no one even heard a whisper of it in India. The year 1818 A. D., in which was made the treaty with the Bhopal State by the English Government, saw the downfall of the power of the Nedjedian insurgents. It is strange then, who introduced Wahabiism into India and who called himself a Wahabi? When, where, and by whom was *jihád* carried on?

In the days of the Indian Mutiny soldiers and troopers had the seals and signatures of some of the Maulvis forcibly impressed upon the *masala* of *jihad* and threateningly obtained *fatwás* written out by the latter. Those who refused were put to the sword and their houses looted. These Maulvis were probably the same persons who at the present day are the deadly enemies of the *Ahl-e-Sunnat* and *Ahl-e-Hadis*, and who perforce call them Wahabis.

Those persons who have brought criminal cases in Government Courts of Justice from Delhi down to Calcutta, and obtained awards of punishment, against people not *Mukallids* of the *Hanafia* church or any other, but who say '*Amín*'* loudly in their prayers and lift up both hands at the time of the *rúkú*†, are beings who have their minds full of mischief and who do not desire religious liberty and the peace of the country, agreeably with the intentions of Government and

---

* The same as the English Amen!
† Bowing the head in humility and reverence, in prayer.

the *Ahl-e-Sunnat* respectively. Those persecuted people, the followers of the *Hadis* and the *Korán*—perforce called Wahabis, a name they do not like to be applied to them—are in the observance of their religious rites, in conformity with the wishes of the English Government. None of them has complained up to this day, in any town in any English Court of Justice, that the Musalmans of a certain town, quarter or mosque, do not say *Amín* loudly and raise their hands in their prayers; and that they should therefore be punished or ordered not to enter a mosque. Whenever and wherever such a complaint has been laid, it has been brought forward by the *Ahl-e-bidat* and not by the *Ahl-e-Hadis*.

Thus the destroyers of peace and security are those persons who designate, as Wahabis, the opponents of their *Khás* religion;* and not the *Mohaddises*.

The authors of the *Sihah Sitta*, viz., six correct books of the *Hadis*, were the guides of the *Ahl-e-Sunnat* and *Jamaat*. A period of one thousand years, more or less, has elapsed since their death. All the succeeding *Mohaddises* have been following their footsteps, and believe in no religion, be it *Hambli* the religion of the Nedjedians, or *Hanafi* the religion of the Sultans of Turkey. Notwithstanding the *masala* of *jihád* occurs in all the six *Hadises*, published at various times with the knowledge and information of the British Government, in the different towns and provinces of India, and the extensive circulation they have had to this day, still none of those who derive the articles of their faith and the rules of their conduct from them alone, has ever raised the standard of *jihád*. On the contrary, the followers of those books have ever been noted for their avoiding the society of kings and great men and passing their lives in retirement. And those kings who fought with their religions adversaries were not *Mohaddises*, but were fettered to the doctrines of a *Khás* religion.

---

* A particular and a newly set up form of faith, not quite in conformity with that taught by the *Hadis* and the *Korán*.

Is it just to call the *Muhaddises* and the *Sunnis* Wahabis and then take the term in the sense of rebellion and *jihád*? Rather this title should have been given to those men who are the followers of the *Hanafi, Shafai,* and other creeds, and who pass their days and nights in ridiculing the *Ahl-e-Hadis.* They whom we call the *Mukallids* and the *Ahl-e-bidat,* are the greatest opponents of the Christian faith.

According to the correspondence in the *Times of India* true *Islám* is that which has obtained since twelve hundred years, a fact not true of Wahabiism. We tread in the course of the religion twelve hundred years old—a religion that has not undergone any subsequent modifications.

People have derived thousands of new ideas from *Islám*—ideas not found in it before—as for instance, one is that of rebellion termed by them the *jihád* of *Shara.* Whereas the meaning of the term *jihad* is what I have already given above, and what Syed Ahmad Khan Bahadur has mentioned in his reply to Dr. Hunter's; and not that which they have moulded and invented out of their brains. Dreading by an overt act of rebellion to draw the vengeance of the English Government upon their own heads, they have with a view of destroying the public peace in a covert manner, hit upon the plan of fixing the charge of Wahabiism upon persons whom they well know to be the *Ahl-e-Hadis;* and thus set the Government itself against them. They wish that the same religious bigotry, the same individual imitation, and the same ancestral spite and ignorance that have prevailed from time immemorial, should continue undiminished; and that the comfort and general security consequent on religious toleration and bestowed by the Government on the Indian subjects be altogether destroyed. They also wish that all Musalmans should follow a *Khás* religion, show as much of bigotry as they can to Government, and on a suitable opportunity cause disturbance like that during the Mutiny.

This conduct of theirs resembles that of a thief brow-beating a *kotwal*,* instead of being himself snubbed.

The case of Kári Abdur Rahman of Panipat, is very startling to me. He, just like the *mukallids* and the *bidatis* who have nicknamed the followers of the *Hadis* and the *Koran*, Wahabis, and attached the mischief wrought by themselves to the skirt of their garment, has written a pamphlet known as *Kashaf-ul-Hejáb* (The removal of a Veil), and published at Lakhnow in 1298 A. H., in which he says that those who declare themselves *Mohaddises* and followers of the *Hadis* and the *Koran*, are *Rafzi Shias*, and use those sacred names as a subterfuge to cause the people to err. He tauntingly writes that I act according to the English laws. His words are :—

"He has made liquor very current. It is openly bought and sold. Acting probably in obedience to the saying 'People follow the ways of their Kings,' duties upon all sorts of articles have been legalized according to the English laws. The Nawáb Wála Jáh levies from the ryots registration fees, stamp fees and different kinds of collection fees, just in accordance with the same laws. All such fees and charges are apparently tyrannical. Now what doubt is there in this sect being *Rafzis*. It has nothing to say against the Hindus, the Christians, or other infidels; but whenever it hears the name of an *Ahl-e-Mazhab*,† it gets mightily enraged."

The above quoted statement is worth the notice of the Government of India. It shows that the charge of Wahabiism against the *Ahl-e-Hadis* is untrue. But it declares that those persons who call themselves the *Ahl-e-Hadis* and consider faithlessness, religious bigotry, misdeeds and rebellion, enormous sins, are really *Rafzis*. It also proves the fact that

---

* The chief officer of the police for a city or town. A police Inspector.

† One who follows a religion ; a *Mokallid*. Here the word indicates a person whose religion is not that of the *Ahl-e-Hadis*.

the mischief-mongers and the enemies of the peace and liberty of mankind, are men who are the *Mukallids* of a *Khás* religion: as for instance, the author of the above-mentioned pamphlet himself who delights in being a *Hanafi*, unlike those persons who rejecting the term Wahabi, have chosen to be called *Sunnis* and *Ahl-e-Hadis*. The latter consider it wrong and a great sin to look out for the acquisition of power, to spread tumult and religious fanaticism in the world, and, out of private grudge and hatred to become the enemy of all.

Nurul Anwar, an Urdu newspaper published in the Nizami Press, dated the 15th *Shauwal** 1298 A. H., copies the following item of news from the *Fortnightly Review* of 1881 A. D.:—

"It appears from the recent Census that all the Mahomedans are seventeen crores and fifty lakhs in number. Of them fourteen crores and fifty lakhs are *Sunnis;* one crore and fifty lakhs, *Shias;* and Wahabis eighty lakhs. Indian Musalmans, subject to the British Government, are four crores in number."

This is a proof that the Indian Musalmans are not Wahabis. And this is quite true, because the term Wahabi was never known before in India. The inhabitants of Mecca and Medina had in 1760 A. D. originated the name for the Nedjedians. But in 1818 A. D. a stop was put to the Wahabi rising.

The Musalmans of Turkey are *Hanafis;* those of Egypt, *Shafais;* those of the west *Malikis;* and those of Damascus &c., *Hamblis*. The *Ahl-e-Sunnat* obey the *Koran* and the *Hadis*. The Musalmans of Persia are *Shias*, and those of Yaman and the adjacent countries, are partly *Zaidis* and

---

* The tenth month of the Mahomedan year, on the first day of which the festival of *Id* is celebrated with great rejoicings, being the first day after *Ramzan*, the month of Fast. It is customary at this festival to make presents to friends and relations.

partly *Mohaddises.* The Musalmans of Muscat are *Kharjis.*
The Indian Musalmans are mostly *Hanafis,* partly *Shias,* and
a very few of them *Ahl-e-Hadis.* There are separate *Mosallas** for each of the four sects of *Islam* in the holy city of
Mecca. The Meccans are opposed to the Wahabis of Nedjed.

Then what authority is there for considering the number
of Wahabis to be eighty lakhs? Such reports and prevalent
rumours very often prove to be utterly unfounded. Mutual
hatred often impel people to calumniate one another. He
that is possessed of sound wisdom should here be thankful
to Government that it does not punish any one on the mere
fact of his being called a Wahabi, until some guilt as that of
rebellion and *jihád* is proved against him. As a proof
of the allegation that Government has nothing to do with a
Wahabi but with a rebel and a *jihádi*† it is sufficient to cite
the case of Syed Ahmad Khan, C. S. I., who claims to be a
Wahabi; but the intention of Government, notwithstanding,
is to daily advance him to emoluments and honours.

Any one be he a Hindu or a Mahomedan—no matter if
the world does not call him a Wahabi but gives him a different name—is sure to meet with a merited punishment, if he
proves himself disloyal to Government by open acts of sedition. And those who confess to their being Wahabis or are so
named by others, can never be called to account until they
are guilty of some rebellious deeds. This is perfect justice.
This statement is specially true of the *Ahl-e-Hadis* in general,
be they the Indians or residents of other countries.

With respect to the Musalman Chiefs of India, Wahabism—nay, even a thought of it—cannot be entertained.
Had any of them been Wahabis, they would surely have
committed misdeeds during the Mutiny. Whereas the marks
of loyalty shown by the Bhopal State and others during that

---

* Carpets to pray on.
† One who makes a *jihád.*

time, are well known to Government. As a reward for the assistance in men and money, Government granted to this State the Pargana of Bairasya* yielding a revenue of one lakh per annum. Four years ago when the news of the proclamation of war with Cabul, reached Bhopal through the Sehore Agency, Her Highness the Nawab Sháh Jahán Bégam, the Ruler of the territory, made various good arrangements and proclaimed that no Turk, Arab, or any other foreigner should sojourn in the town. So, that order is still enforced and carried out. She wrote to Government saying that the Bhopal Contingent and the Bhopal force were at its service, and that the State was all ready with its assistance in men, money and munitions. For four long years the Bhopal force was stationed at the Sehore Cantonment and did all the duties of the Contingent. Her Highness the Begam and myself contributed our respective shares to the fund for the maintenance of widows of the soldiers that fell in the Cabul Campaign. Whatever be the order of Government at whatever time, it is immediately carried out; and precedence is always given to it over all the business of the State. It is provided in the Statute of this State that any *amil*,† *thanadar*,‡ or *mohtamim*§ of a Court of Justice, delaying in carrying out a Government order, shall be subjected to a just punishment.

Our religious impression is that whatever tends to mischief in the government of a country, or results in the violation of a promise or destruction of the safety of the subjects, is opposed to *Islám*. It is highly sinful to try for the acquisi-

---

* This pargana was granted by the British Government to the State of Bhopal, on 27th December 1860 at a Durbar held by the Governor-General at Jabalpur, for services rendered during the Mutiny of 1857.

† A superintendent of the finances; Revenue Collector.

‡ In the State of Bhopal this word signifies a Police Inspector with small judicial powers.

§ A superintendent or head of a department.

tion of power and overspread the earth with wickedness and war. Rigorous religious opinions, following a *khas* religion, overthrowing liberty, telling lies, deceiving, and bribery and corruption, are strictly forbidden in *Islám*.

I have not, within my experience, found any sect which is a greater friend, a better desirer of the safety and repose of the ryots, and a better appreciator of the British Rule, than that which is known as the *Ahl-e-Sunnat* and *Hadis;* and which practising no *khas* religion and entertaining no prejudice against any faith, prays and fasts and performs all the other duties of its creed, quite content with the existing means of its livelihood.

According to the *Korán* and the *Hádís*, it is an enormous sin to do mischievous acts, warrant bloodshed, seize upon other's wealth, dishonour a person, violate a promise, and think it good to rebel against the Government.

There is no mention of the term 'Wahabi' anywhere in the Islamic books. It has come into force since the time of Mahomed *bin* Abdul Wahab of Nedjed, just as *Bábia*, the name of a sect which, forty years ago, fought with the kings of Persia and others, originated in the former country. The religion of the above-named Nedjedian, the invader of the Bohras and the Bedouins, was *Hambli*. Books treating of the religion are not current in India. Especially those composed by Mahomed *bin* Abdul Wahab himself, have scarcely ever been seen by any one, not to speak of their existence, their perusal and their circulation. The year 1760 A. D. was the beginning and 1881 A. D. the end, of Wahabiism. Thus this religious conflict lasted for a period of fifty-eight years in Nedjed, with the result that most people became the enemies of the new sect. Sixty-three years have now elapsed since the voice of it was last heard.

My lamented father in his treatise called the *Hidáyatul-Mominín* (A guide for Moslems), compiled by him in the year 1249 A. H. and printed in Calcutta during his lifetime, condemns the practice of worshipping *tázias* as heretical. This treatise of his obtained a very extended circulation and went through several editions. A copy of the edition printed again very recently in the year 1298 A. H.. at the Farutí Press, Delhi, has come to us at Bhopal. About the heretical *tázia* worship, he writes :—

"When some foolish persons hear others prohibit the worship of *tázias*, they accuse them of Wahabiism, because, the Wahabis used to prohibit such a worship. In answer to this I say that whatever I have been telling you against, has its evils mentioned in the *Koran* and the *Hadis*. We do not even talk of Wahabis, nor do we consider their words reliable. If you still persist in calling us Wahabis, you betray your own ignorance. If the term 'Wahabi' means one who removes *shirk* and *bidat*, and acts according to the teachings of the *Korán* and the *Hadís*, then we have no objection to be so named. As observed by Imam Sháfai that if by *Rifz** is meant love and affection for the descendants of Mahomed, I would like to be a *Ráfzí*."

The above passage occurs in the recent edition of the book in pages 42 and 43. It is plain from this that the *Ahl-e-Hadís* are not Wahabis. On the other hand the religion of the *Ahl-e-Sunnat* and *Hadis* is dated the very day when *Islám* began in the world. No history proves the fact of any one calling a *Mohaddis* a Wahabi; or of any *Mohaddis* ever perpetuating mischief in any country, or waging *jihád* with any of the kings or *Hákims*. On the contrary, all the books, biographies and histories agree in saying that the life led by the *Mohaddises*, has always been one of retirement from the world, of prayer and of devotion to learning. Some of these were dervises, called *Súfis*,† *Fakirs* and *Záhids*.‡ They

---

* Schism, heresy.

† A sect of freethinkers among the Musalmans.

‡ Devout persons.

did not visit worldly men. Some of them were also *álims* devoted to tuition and instruction, composition and compilation. They avoided the service and society of kings.

What now remains to be told is that some of their doctrines and rules of faith coincide with those of the Nedjedians. The truth of it is that there is no religion in the world, be it true or false, some of whose precepts do not agree with those of others. For instance, theft, adultery, oppression, falsehood, bloodshed, and rebellion, have, in all religious denominations, been considered as vices; and that clearing this earth from wickedness, securing the safety of ryots, almsgiving, and bestowing bread and clothes upon the needy, are good in the eyes of all.

There are some precepts and articles of faith in the *Korán* and the *Hadis*, which are all in accordance with those in the Old and the New Testaments. Again there are rules in the Islamic faith which Government approves of in the administration of the country. Hence from this particular agreement of some parts a man can never be doomed to the name which is the name of the founder of a religion.

We consider Moses and Jesus prophets in the same manner as we consider our prophet the apostle of God. We cannot for this belief be thought either Jews or Christians. The *Shiás* raise their hands during prayer, as also the *Ahl-e-Hadis*; but for this no one has to this day called the latter *Shiás*. The *Shiás* also consider *jihád* to be imperative on the appearance of Imam Mehdi. They are nevertheless not known as Wahabis.

'*Asar-ul-Adhár*, a book compiled by Salím Khori, a Christian, and *Almirrat-ul-Waziata*, another book compiled by Colonel Yousecandeck (?), give the following particulars with regard to the Wahabis:—

Saud of Nedjed fought with the Bohrás and the Bedouins of Arabia whose reputation as Mahomedans was only nominal, and not with any Hindu Rajas or the English

Government. He took all the Mahomedans of the world to be infidels, and, for this reason, considered it right to kill them and plunder their properties. So much so that on the fall of the sacred cities, Mecca and Medina, complaint reached the Sultan of Turkey. However in the time of Mahomed Ali Pasha, he was defeated, taken prisoner and, bound in chains, was sent to Constantinople where he died in prison.

The Mahomedan world is safe since that day. The *Ahl-e-Sunnat* and *Hadis* of the present day do not at all act up to his teachings, because Saúd followed a *khas* religion which they do not believe in. Their religion is the *Hadis* by which they principally act. They fly thousands of miles off from mischievous deeds, deny Wahabiism and startle at the name. They consider Wahabiism heresy in religion, call themselves *Sunnis* and give the name 'Ahl-e-Sunnat' to their sect.

For this reason to call the *Mohaddis* and the *Ahl-e-Sunnat* by the name 'Wahabis' and understand by that term 'rebels' and '*jihádis*', is unwise and unfounded. The *Hanafis* call themselves *Hanafis*; the *Hamblis*, *Hamblis*; the *Zaidis*, *Zaidís*; and the *Shiás*, *Shiás*. In the same manner do the Christians and the Jews declare themselves Christians and Jews respectively. But no *Mohaddis* calls himself a Wahabi: and how can he approve of that new appellation in respect of himself, when he dislikes the terms *Hanafi*, *Sháfai*, and *Máliki*, quite ancient words, to be applied to himself.

The religion of the *Hadis* is dated one thousand years before the Wahabiism of Nedjed which has sprung up only now, one thousand years afterwards. This name does not suit the *Ahl-e-Hadis* by any manner of means. On the other hand, the difference between the *Ahl-e-Hadis* and the *Ahl-e-Mazhab* is the same as that between the Protestants and the Roman Catholics; as Syed Ahmad Khan, C. S. I. has written in his reply to Dr. Hunter.

We need not be afraid of rebellion from the *Ahl-e Ha-*

dis. They scrupulously keep themselves always apart from mischief and save others from it by their words and writings. They are the lovers of peace and safety. It is a different thing altogether when one incited by hatred and enmity, calls another a Wahabi, a *Ráfzi*, or a *Kharji;* and imposing upon the *Hákims* by a stroke of cunning and deceit, tries to give him a bad character.

Just now a gentleman presented me with a copy of the *Civil and Military Gazette*, dated the 3rd February, 1882, containing an article in page 3, which is worthy of great reflection. I therefore quote it in its entirety:

"The current number of the *Ishaatus-sunnat* contains a long leading article under the heading 'Wahabis,' attempting to prove that the Wahabis of India (who in the article under notice are styled as *Mowahideens*) are as good and loyal subjects of the Queen as any other section of the Mahomedan community. The article in question commences by stating that the name 'Wahabi' is regarded by the *Mowahideens* in the same light as that of *bidati*—that is, superstitious—by the Sunnis. The reasons why they do so regard it are many. In the first place the word—whatever be its meaning from a religious and literary point of view—has long been associated with disloyalty, as the Sunnis have long laboured to impress on the rulers of the country, that *Mowahideens* of India, like the Wahabis of Hazara and other frontier tribes, are the enemies of order and peace, and that they hold it lawful to make *jehád*, or religious war, against the British Government. That the *Mowahideens* have cleared themselves of this most malicious and serious charge, is evident from the fact that, in 1875 Moulvi Mahomed Hossein, one of the leading and most influential *Mowahideens* of Lahore, when asked to give his opinion as to whether it was lawful to take up arms against the British, replied that a religious war against the British Government, or any other Government which allowed perfect freedom in religious matters, so far from being countenanced by the Mahomedan Law of *jehád*, was opposed to the doctrines of *Islám*. In proof of his assertion he compiled a treatise entitled 'Jehád,' in which he most ably and conclusively demonstrated that making *jehád* against a Government like the British was unlawful and equal to a rebellion towards a lawful king, and those who took any part in such a war deserved to be treated as rebels. This pamphlet he caused to be circulated among a large number of the most learned Maulvis of the Panjab and of other provinces, for the purpose of eliciting their opinions on the subject, and of ascertaining whether the quotations made by him in support of his statements were from competent authorities, or otherwise. All Maulvis among whom the treatise in question was circulated, unanimously testified their entire concurrence with the opinions of Maulvi Mahomed Hossein, and declared his authorities to be unimpeachably trustworthy, putting down their signatures and seals to the pamphlet as a mark of concurrence with its contents. The learned Maulvi further offered to undertake a mission to Hazara, for the purpose of impressing on the minds of the Wahabis of that place that disturbances raised by them on the frontier, and which they regarded as *jehád* against the unbelievers, were in direct contravention of the religious principles of Islám, and that they would be responsible for any lives that might be lost in such disturbances. The matter was brought to the notice of Sir Henry Davies, the then Lieutenant-Governor of the Punjab, who thanked the Maulvi for this proof of loyalty to Government, but thought it unadvisable to send a mission of the sort proposed by Maulvi Mahomed Hossein to Hazara. The *Mowahideens* of Lahore then petitioned Sir Henry Davies to issue an order prohibiting the Sunnis and others to call the *Mowahideens* by the name of Wahabi. This request was granted, and a cirular was accordingly issued to the effect that, as Government had no doubt as to the loyalty of the *Mowahi-*

deens of India, who, unlike the Wahabis of Hazara, were faithful to the British Government, they should not be called Wahabis.

"Secondly—the epithet Wahabi represents them to be the followers of a notorious Arabian agitator named Muhammad Ben Abdul Wahab, who raised the standard of revolt in Nejid in 1212 A. H. That they are not the followers of Abdul Wahab may reasonably be inferred from the fact that Abdul Wahab belonged to the Hanbuli sect of Mahomedans—one of the four great sects into which Mahomedans are divided. The *Mowahideens* do not belong to any of the sects named above, simply because none of them existed during the lifetime of the Prophet whom they follow in the mode of worship. The only difference between the *Mowahideens* and other sects of Mahomedans is that they believe in the Koran and the trustworthy traditions of the Prophet, and nothing else. They do not at all believe in the saints and *walis*; they regard grave-worship as a superstition of the most absurd kind and opposed to the teaching of the Koran. They think it useless to give charity, offer up prayers, or feed the *Mullás* on behalf of the dead, and other absurdities which the Mahomedans appear to have borrowed from the Hindus. Besides, there is no work from the pen of Abdul Wahab in use among the Maulvis of India, from which the Wahabis may be supposed to have derived the principles of their faith. Nor are the Wahabis of India in the habit of going to Nejid or corresponding with the Nejidis. Under these circumstances, the writer of the article under notice argues that it is a pity the *Mowahideens* of India should be called by a name which signifies disloyalty to Government, and which represents them to be the followers of an agitator with whom they have no sympathy whatever."

Now I pray God to save us from the habits, customs, society, and love of those persons in respect of whom the angels have said: "Why art Thou creating on the earth such men as will be mischievous in the world and spill blood." May God always save us from turbulence and disaffection, take us away in our full faith, and pardon all our sins known and unknown, that have offended Him or may offend Him in future.

THE END.

CONCLUSION.

Although in this treatise I have written at length the history of Wahabiism and the *masala* of *jihád* in its present acceptation, still I have not separately mentioned the commands regarding the mode of procedure one should adopt at the time of rebellion, according to the religion of the *Mowahhids* and the *Ahl-e-Hadis*.

In this conclusion I purpose putting down the translation of some of the *Hadises*, which shall show what part Musalman *Mowahhids* should play on the occurrence of anarchy and sedition.

It is necessary to write this here, because the world is near its end, and the time that has yet to come is very short compared to what has already passed. The time of the ancient Mahomedans extended, as it were, between morning and *asar;* and the period of the Mahomedans of the present age, extends beween *asar* and sunset. Out of this period thirteen hundred years have already passed away. So the world has now already approached its completion and the Judgment Day is upon our heads. Although the exact time of that occurrence is not known to any of the prophets, saints, religious divines, and pious men, except God himself; still so far is known for certain that if the day of the general resurrection was near before, it must be nearer now; and that it will come all at once presaged by thousands of evils. As, for instance, the occurrences of hundreds of evils and disturbances in these last thirteen hundred years of the Hijra are well-known with exactness as to their dates, from Histories and Travels. They have been fully detailed in the book called *Hojájul Karama*. Other disturbances are seen and heard to follow each other uninterruptedly day by day. The present age has been thought to be the age of numerous commotions.

When this age is the age of tumult, it is necessary to know the commands according to which every Mahomedan should act and refrain from combining with the turbulent and the mischievous, during the time of actual disturbance.

If any Mahomedan does not acquaint himself with the strife and civil commotions—foretold by our Prophet long before—that are to happen among this favoured people, and does not act according to the behests of prophecy, it is his fault and not a defect in *Islám*.

Now listen! Hozaifa *bin* Yamán, a *Sahábí**, says that he heard the Prophet of God (may God be gracious unto him and his posterity) saying " *Fitnas* are represented upon the mind like a mat work. The heart which drinks in a *fitna* has therefore a black spot in it, and that which does not has a white one. So that two kinds of hearts are produced. The one is white like marble, which cannot be affected by a *fitna* as long as the earth and the sky exist. The other is black like ashes and resembles a reverse basin which empties every thing that it contains. Such a heart does not know good, nor desists from bad acts; but knows only those that it has imbibed out of interested desires." Related in *Muslim*.

Fitna means 'examination' and 'trial,' also to 'err' and 'cause to err.' It is manifest from the above *Hadís* that the heart which does not imbibe a *fitna* is white, pure, clean and enlightened; and that which does is vicious, black and turned upside down.

In another *Hadís* the Prophet says that faithlessness is also a *fitna*. In a third *Hadís* it is mentioned:—

Hozaifa says, " People used to ask the Prophet of God about virtues, whereas I asked him about vices, lest I should be infected with one. I told him—we were immersed in ignorance and that God sent this good, *i. e.*, *Islím* to us. Will this good be followed by wickedness? He said—yes, it will be. I questioned—will that wickedness be again followed

---

* A companion of the Prophet.

by virtue? He said—yes, but it will be tinged with impurity. I asked—what sort of impurity will it be? He replied—such men will appear as will tread a different path from that which I have shown, and act contrary to my ordinances. Some persons will understand their speech and some not. I said—will vices again follow this virtue? He replied—yes they will. Some will call people to the door of the Hell, and no sooner will they listen to their voice than they shall be hurled into it. I asked him—who are they? He said—their skin and hair will be like ours and they will speak our tongue. I asked him—what should I do if they be contemporary with me? He said—stick to the company of Musalmans and their *Imám*. I said—if such a congregation and an *Imám* cannot be had what should I do? He said—live apart from those people. Though you should be put to the necessity of cutting the roots of trees with your own teeth, entailing so much labour and pain as to cause your death, still you should continue steadfast in this course."

In *Muslim* the same *riwáet** occurs in this manner:— The Prophet said "Such *Imáms* or spiritual guides shall appear after me as will not tread in my faith. Some of them will be such as will possess the heart of Satan in a human body." Hozaifa asked, "What should I do if I happen to meet with such people." The Prophet said, "Listen to the commands of your *Hákim*. Should he strike you on your back and seize upon your properties, still you should obey and listen to him."

It is apparent from the above *Hadis* that virtue and vice are found together; that vice follows virtue, and virtue vice; that we should not listen to the voices of those vicious and turbulent souls who, coming out under the garb of good people, mislead and impose upon others; and that we should seclude ourselves from tumults and pass our days in retire-

---

* That which is related; a tradition.

ment, in order that we may be safe from *fitnas* and live in perfect security.

The present age is such that it neither has an *Imám* nor a *Jamaat* of Musalmans. *Jamaat* means unity of hearts and tongues. In lieu of such a union, the Mahomedans of the present day have thousand hearts and thousand tongues. One is thirsty for the blood of another. Retirement is therefore calculated to secure protection of life, preserve the faith and produce security. If one is not safe in a town he should retire to a village and pass his days under the shade of a tree; but never should he join in sedition and turbulence.

Abu Horaira relates that the Prophet said: "Be quick in performing your duties before the appearance of those *fitnas* which, resembling the parts of a dark night, will make men that are *Momins* (Musalmans) in the morning, *Káfirs* in the evening, and those that are *Momins* in the evening *Káfirs* in the morning. People will sell their religion for petty worldly interests." That is to say, the Islamic faith will become so weak in the last part of the age that a man will be Musalman in one hour and *Káfir* in another; and that he will not be settled in anything.

Our eyes and ears are witnesses of the fact that some persons have become Christians, then Musalmans, and then Christians again; that some *Shias* becoming *Sunnis*, have, after a few days, gone back to their former faith; and that many Hindus and Christians after accepting Mahomedanism have returned to their old creeds. These changes are also a kind of *fitna* and argue the nearness of the day of judgment and corroborate the truths of what our prophet has already foretold.

Now listen to the command as to what we should do during the times of *fitnas*.

Abu Horaira mentions that the Prophet said: "The time is near of serious and innumerable *fitnas* manifesting themselves. During such times a sitting man is better than one standing, a standing better than one walking and a walking man better than one running. In short, whoever shall peep towards a *fitna* is sure to be drawn towards it. So that should a person find a place of refuge and shelter, he should never give it up."

In *Muslim* the same *Hadis* occurs thus:—*Fitnas* will take place. A sleeping man is better than one awake, a waking man is better than one standing, and a standing better than one who is exerting. So that if one should get an asylum and a place of refuge, he should stand by it." It appears from this *Hadis* that it is right to live as much apart from *fitnas* as is possible for us to do so; that one should take refuge from them wherever refuge can be had; and that he should never commingle himself into *fitnas*, but save himself from them as much as possible.

Abi Bakr writes that the Prophet said: "The time of the appearance of great *fitnas* is nigh. During those *fitnas* a sitting man shall be better than one walking, and a walking shall be better than those that will be running. Should these *fitnas* actually occur, then those that have camels should join their camels, those that have goats should join their goats, and those that have lands should go to their lands." Upon this one man asked: "What should a man do if he did not possess camels, goats or lands." The Prophet answered: "He should take his sword and blunt the edge of it with a piece of stone and thus would he be all safe." He further said, "O God, bear witness that I have communicated thy commands, *i. e.*, three times have I delivered thy commands, to thy people!" A man asked him "O Prophet of God! what will become of the man who forcibly takes me from one party to another and strikes me with his sword, or kills me with his arrow." He replied, "He shall take his and thy sins upon his head and be among those doomed for hell." Related in *Muslim*.

It appears, this *Hadis* strictly prohibits participation in a *fitna* either willingly or by another forcing us to it. If a man that has been forcibly enlisted into a party or faction, should happen to be killed by the hand and with a weapon of another, he would be perfectly sinless, because he did not join the *fitná* at his own free will. The crime of taking him to the *fitna*, of killing him or causing him to kill others, should be upon the neck of those who took, or, caused another to take, his life when he was in a helpless condition. And the reason of our Prophet dictating three times the command of God, was to inculcate adherence to it and to nothing else.

Abi Said Khudrí relates that the Prophet said: "The time is near when the goats will be regarded the best property of the Musalmans, when the latter shall follow the former upon mountain peaks and near waterpools, to escape from *fitnas* with their faith." Mentioned in *Bokhári*.

The meaning of this *Hadis* is that, in order to escape from *fitnas*, it is right to betake oneself to jungles, streams and mountains. It is not good to precipitate oneself into a *fitna* and thus get entangled in turbulence and sedition.

But how pitiable is the state of the Mahomedans of the present day, who, instead of escaping, happen, somehow or other, to mix themselves in thousands of *fitnas;* and who, regarding the wars of conquest and those waged between one *Hakim* and another, in the light of *jehád* or virtuous acts, espouse the cause of one of the parties. The consequence of this has often been the loss of all worldly interests over and above the loss of faith that on the very first day of their disaffection bade adieu to them.

Abi Horaira mentions that the Prophet said: "As the time of this and the next world will near each other, learning will be scarce, *fitnas* will appear, the hearts of the people will be miserly, and bloodshed will be rife."

These signs are being manifested in these days. *Fitnas* are so abundant that not a town or house is safe from them. Books treating on different subjects exist by thousands, but learned men are nowhere to be found. If one in a thousand happens to be acquainted to some extent with the *word* religion, he seldom has the desire of bringing his knowledge to practice. Stinginess has grown so general that one grudges the generosity of others—being himself generous and munificent is out of the question. Subscriptions and solicitations for alms, answer much purpose now-a-days. It is hard to spend even a cowrie from one's own pocket.

Zobair *bin* Adí says that he complained to Anas *bin* Malik of the tyranny of Hujjáj *bin* Yusuf. Anas replied: "Endure it. No hard time shall come upon you, though the succeeding period will always be harder than the preceding. You should be so resigned as ultimately to meet your Preserver. I have heard your Prophet say all this." Narrated in *Bokhári*.

When we reflect upon the period that has elapsed since the time of our Prophet, every century, every decade, and every day of it, appears to have been filled with ever-increasing evils detrimental to both our worldly and spiritual concerns; and that the succeeding ages present a worse appearance than the preceding ones. The times of the descent of Jesus Christ and the appearance of Imam Mehdi, with other *Hadises* relating to them, form an exception to the above *Hadis*. May God soon bring them both to our sight, the one from the sky and the other from the earth.

Hozaifa says: "By God, I remember to have been told by the Prophet the names of those disturbers of the peace, their fathers' and their tribes' names, that shall be fomenting sedition to the last day, and the number of whose followers is three hundred or more; but I cannot say whether my friends remember it or have wilfully forgotten it." Related in *Abu Dáúd*.

In the *Hadis* of Saubán it is related thus—the Prophet said: "If I am at all anxious about my people, it is owing to the misguiding *Imams* and no others. When my people will put by their swords they shall not take them up even to the Judgment Day." Narrated in *Abu Dáúd* and *Tirmizi*.

It appears that this *Hadis* predicts the appearance of such *Imams* as will lead the people astray. As for instance, those who during the prevalence of *fitnas* give the order for *jehad* and thereby destroy altogether the interests of the poor, illiterate Mahomedans, both here and in the world to come; knowing full well that the riot, the tumult, and the violence got up here and there by wicked and dissolute fellows, are, according to our religious laws, *fitnas* and no *jehád*. Rather than dilating upon the virtues of *jehád* and participating and causing others to join, in a *fitna*, they had better desist and and cause others to do the same. We have been talking here of *Imáms*. Those who are not *Imáms*, nor possess any knowledge or excellence, but who having read only two or three books in Urdu and Persian, make themselves known as Mullas and Maulvis, and endeavour to spoil *Islám* by overt and covert acts of mischief, are really impostors, liars and dissemblers. They have been alluded to in other *Hadises*.

The Prophet has already foretold that there shall be thirty *Dajjals* among his people, up to the end of the world. So that some of these have already appeared in the world, and the rest are appearing. Even at the present day there are one or two persons of the above description. May God save us from all violence and evil-doing.

Another meaning implied from the above *Hadis* is, that bloodshed shall be rife among the Musalmans. Historical books corroborate the fact that in all ages have the poor and poverty-stricken Mahomedans been put to the sword, and that the Mahomedan kings themselves have fought with one another for love of conquest, and thereby spilt useless blood. Now-a-days bloodshed is committed by the hands of other nations and will continue to the last day. Those persons are safe who, considering it a turbulent act, take refuge from it; and those who participate in it are lost for ever.

Abdullah *bin* Umar *bin* A's says, that the Prophet spoke to him thus: "What would be your fate were you to be cast among bad people like a barley-corn among chaff,—people whose words, promises and faith will be quite mixed up and be different from one another?" He asked what he was to do then. The Prophet said: "It is proper for you to stick to that which you know to be true, and give up that which you do not know. Save your life and mix not with the common people." Another version of the same is given thus:—"Keep yourself at home. Rein your tongue. Stick to good things and leave off the bad. Better your own life and do not concern yourself with the affairs of the vulgar." Related in *Tirmizi* and *Sehha*.

Abu Musa says that the Prophet said: "Disturbances like the parts of a dark night will occur before the general resurrection. During their prevalence a man that is a Mahomedan in the morning will be a *Káfir* by the evening; and one that is a true believer in the evening will be an unbeliever by the morning. Then a man who is sitting is better than one who is standing, and one who is walking is better than one who is running. During such disturbances break your bows and cut asunder their strings and blunt the edge of your swords, so that should one come to kill you, you should behave like the better of the two sons of Adam." Mentioned in *Abú Dáúd*.

In another *Hadis* it occurs that the companions of the Prophet asked him what his command was with respect to themselves? He said: "Retire to the old matting of your own house, *i. e.*, do not go out from your house, as an old matting is not removed from under a good carpeting." Another version is: "Retire to your house, *i. e.*, do not go out lest you should be involved in a disturbance."

The two sons of Adam alluded to above were Cain and Abel. Cain slew his brother Abel who was thus the injured party. During disturbances be like him injured and oppressed; but do not be an injurer or oppressor yourself. Do not kill any one. Rather break your weapons and blunt their edges. If any one should come and beat you bear it and die.

Abú Horaira relates that the Prophet said: "The time of the occurrence of a *fitna* is very near. Whoever shall peep towards it—no matter if he be deaf, dumb or blind—is sure to be drawn towards it. To talk too much about it is equal to wielding a sword." Related in *Abú Dáúd*.

That is to say, the sin and fault, the consequence of verbal participation in dangerous insurrections, are as egregious as the using of a sword. This means that we should not take part in them even with our tongue—to join in them with our hearts and hands is out of the question. Prticipation in them with our tongue is effected by talking of them, giving one's opinion on them, proclaiming them and speaking about them before others, hearing accounts of them and being desirous of ascertaining the truth about them. Of course it does not matter if one hears of them with a view to escape.

Mekdád *bin* Aswad says that he heard the Prophet saying: "The virtuous are those who have nothing to do with *fitnas*." This he repeated three times and then said "And pitiable are the circumstances of those who unknowingly get entangled in *fitnas* and bear them patiently—pitiable because they could not keep themselves apart from them." Related in *Abú Dáúd*.

The following occurs in the bulky *Hadis* of Abi Horaira :—"The last day will not come until thirty impostors, *Dajjáls*, have been born. They will think themselves prophets."

It is said some people have, in these days, claimed to be prophets. Whether this report is true or not, is known to God alone.

The following *Hadis* traced to the very source, is mentioned by Hozaifa :—" When a *fitna*, caused by a man, affects his people, his wealth, his feelings, his offsprings and his neighbours, it is atoned for or expiated by prayers, fasts and voluntary alms."

It appears fom this *Hadis* that besides the above-mentioned *fitna*, all others raging like the billows of the sea, are not expiable. To get oneself involved in the latter, is to lose both temporal and spiritual concerns.

In the *Hadis* of Jábir *bin* Samrá occurs the following:— The Prophet said: "Great liars shall appear before the occurrence of the Day of Judgment. Beware of them." Related in *Muslim*.

Abi Horaira writes that the Prophet said: "By God, in whose hands my life is, the world shall not be reduced to nothing until men have passed by graves and rolled themselves upon them ejaculating longing desires—not because of their habit or their faith, but by reason of their misfortune and misery—to be themselves placed in those repositories of the dead." Related in *Muslim*.

Anas (may God be pleased with him) writes that the Prophet said: "Time will get diminished in duration by the approach of the Day of Judgment. So that a year shall be as small as a month, a month as short as a week, a week as short as a day, a day as short as an hour, and an hour as short as a flash of fire." Related in *Tirmizi*.

That is to say, the inherent prosperity of the world will be all gone and the benefits of it all lost. Many illustrations of this are to be met with at the present day.

With regard to his people of the modern times the Prophet has said: "Those of my people will love me most, that will flourish after me. They will long to see me even if it were at the sacrifice of their wealth and all." Related in *Muslim*. (This *Hadis* has been derived from Abi Horaira who again derived it, by successive traditions, from the Prophet himself.)

In the *Hadis* of Máwia occurs: "A certain sect among my people will remain always obedient to God's command. No renegade from that sect, unwilling to assist, shall be able to oppose or injure it, till the divine command or the Judgment Day comes on."

Anas writes that the Prophet said: "The story of my people is the same as that of rain about which it is difficult to tell whether the first or the last is better." Related in *Tirmizi*.

Ali *bin* Hosain writes on an unquestionable authority that the Prophet said: "How can those people be spoiled or ruined that have me for their beginning, Imám Mehdi for their middle, and the Messiah for their end. But in the intervening period a tribe that shall go astray, will appear —a tribe which is not from me, nor I from it." Related by Razin.

The Prophet further said: "To tell the truth, the tribe most liked by me is that which will come after me. They shall receive books which will also become proselytised to the faith their contents teach, along with the tribe. That is to say, receiving the *Korán* and the *Hadis*, the men of the tribe will act up to their teachings as if impelled by something invisible." This points out the excellence of faith created of itself. Related by Baihaki.

Baihaki relates the following on the authority of Abdur Rahman *bin* Alal Hazremi who again traces it, by successive traditions, to the Prophet himself:—"It is very near that a tribe shall appear in the last period of this people, that will be rewarded in the same manner as the first people have been. They will inculcate good lessons and prohibit people to do bad acts. They will fight with the agitators and the malcontents, *i. e.*, the rebels, the *Khárjis*, the *Ráfzis* and the *bidatís*. This fight includes both that with hands and tongues whichever be possible."

In the *Hadis* of Kurra *bin* Aiyas occurs the following:—

"When the Syrians will be destroyed no goodness shall be found in you. A certain band of my people is especially favoured. Till doomsday no one that is against it shall be able to injure it." Related in *Tirmizi* and testified to as correct.

Ibn-ul-Madini the tutor of the author of *Bokhári* a book of great authority, says that the band alluded to above is that of the *Ahl-e-Hadis*, that is to say, the *Ahl-e-Sunnat* and *Jamaat* who have ever been engaged in extirpating Wahabiism and sin from this world and who have distinctly laid down rules what a man should do during troublous times.

Ibn Abbas writes that the Prophet said: " God has forgiven the errors and mistakes inadvertently committed by my people, and the acts they are obliged to do by external pressure." Related by Ibn Maja and Baihaki.

I wish to end this book with the following prayer:—

When Thou hast forgiven, O God, the faults and the mistakes of the Mahomedans and taken away the odium from them, out of Thy grace, liberality and general mercy, forgive the errors, faults and other palpable defects that I may have been guilty of, first in this book in regard to the representation of facts or narrations, and, secondly, in the acts throughout my life from the day of my birth till the present time! Do not apprehend me, O God, for my sins, but end my days with the *Kalemá Shabádat** on my lips, uttered with an ecstasy of devotion and sincerity.

---

* A formula of the Mahomedan confession of faith which, it is believed, if repeated by the dying at the moment of death, is sure to cleanse him from all sins and prepare his way to heaven.

www.ingramcontent.com/pod-product-compliance
Lightning Source LLC
Chambersburg PA
CBHW030352170426
43202CB00010B/1344